# Foundations for the Teaching Church

Grant W. Hanson

# Foundations for the Teaching Church

## Christian Faith, Personal Nurture, & Church Life

Judson Press ® Valley Forge

FOUNDATIONS FOR THE TEACHING CHURCH



**Library of Congress Cataloging-in-Publication Data**

Hanson, Grant W.
Foundations for the teaching church.

Bibliography: p.
1. Christian education—Philosophy. I. Title.
BV1464.H33 1986 207 86-2716
ISBN 0-8170-1096-3


Printed in the U.S.A.

*Dedicated to my former colleagues in the Division of Church Education, Board of Educational Ministries, American Baptist Churches in the U.S.A., who shared in the vision of the teaching church*

# Contents

# Foreword

Grant Hanson has been my friend and colleague for thirty-five years. I know of his personal "journey" in the educational ministry of the church. As pastor, minister of Christian education, area director of Christian education, and national staff person for Christian education, he has lived out what he writes. This is not simply a book. It is a testimony of his concern for the teaching ministry of the church.

Out of his personal commitment he offers us a thorough look at the foundations upon which we build a teaching ministry. Reading this book has given me a sense of personal and professional hope, excitement, and direction.

It is a new day! The struggle between feelings of satisfaction and accomplishment and those of routine and frustration in regard to the church's teaching ministry is responded to if not resolved. This book offers a sense of renewal to the reader—a gift that can permeate one's involvement in the teaching church.

*Foundations for the Teaching Church* is the second* in a series of books designed to help us understand and implement the concept of the teaching church. The contents are both theoretical and practical, dealing with the "why" of what we do as well as the "what." This book is worthy of the time and consideration of all those involved in the educational ministry of the church.

*Foundations for the Teaching Church* has the potential for helping

*The first was *Developing Leadership in the Teaching Church* by Jan Chartier (Judson Press, 1985).

church leaders to see a larger vision of the church's teaching ministry as all that the church is and does. Grant Hanson opens the way for a clearer, if not new, understanding of this vital ministry. We who are leaders of the church's teaching ministry owe him our gratitude.

*John L. "Bud" Carroll*
*Director, Division of Church Education*
*American Baptist Churches*
*Valley Forge, Pennsylvania*

# 1

# The Concept of the Teaching Church

The centrality of the tradition of teaching is apparent throughout the Bible. The story of God's relationship to a special people was passed from generation to generation by a careful oral tradition. Each child was expected to learn the story of how God has been revealed through interactions with persons in times past. The wisdom and experience of the race were part of a heritage that had to be transmitted faithfully to each new generation. The whole community shared the responsibility, and certain persons were designated as teachers.

The transition from the oral tradition to a written record of history did not change the teaching function. When the church came into existence in the first century, it inherited the Jewish Scriptures (Old Testament). To these were added the church's own writings, which in time became the New Testament. The tradition of teaching is long and rich and is built into the very fabric of the community of faith. The continued existence of the church depends upon its faithfulness to the tradition of teaching. Each generation must receive from the previous generation the legacy of the church's faith experience and appropriate it as its own.

This long tradition makes it reasonable to talk about "the teaching church." In using this phrase, one describes the nature of the church in its very essence and differentiates that nature from the simple reference to one function among a variety of functions. Teaching is more than an activity of the church; it is the *fabric* of the church. The church endangers its own existence when it does not remain faithful to its nature as a teaching community.

## The Goal of Ministry

The goal of ministry of the teaching church has been expressed in many ways. All efforts have attempted to describe the hoped-for outcome. The goal is a measuring tool for determining if the church has fulfilled its nature in terms of the mission to which it is called. One goal statement widely used is the one which was developed by a group of Protestant denominations in conjunction with the Cooperative Curriculum Project in the late 1950s and early 1960s. An interpretation of the statement follows.

*The goal of the church's education ministry is*

The starting point for the fulfillment of the church's calling as a teaching community is shared understanding on the part of the congregation about its task. Little will be accomplished unless there can be a clear perception of what is to happen, of an end. Self-understanding is a necessary ingredient for any group that proposes to be true to its own nature. Setting forth the goal provides the means of recognizing when achievement has taken place.

*that all persons*

The teaching church has to have a global perspective. Its concern knows no barriers or limits. Its vision encompasses not simply its own fellowship but the whole world. A strong link joins teaching and evangelism. The Good News is for everyone. The stress is on inclusiveness and universality.

*be aware of God*

The starting point for the redemptive process is that wonderful moment of awareness of the Eternal One confronting persons at the very core of their beings.

*through God's self-disclosure,*

The initiative remains with God who uses both creation and history as arenas of self-revelation. As the writer of Hebrews reminds us, God has spoken in a variety of ways through persons and finally in a Son who reflects the glory and nature of God (Hebrews 1:1-2). The church's record of this revelation is found in its Holy Scriptures.

*especially God's redeeming love as revealed in Jesus Christ,*

The heart of the ministry of the teaching church is the person and work of Jesus Christ. God's redemptive love is experienced through the mediation of this One who entered history and became fully human.

*and, enabled by the Holy Spirit,*

God has a continual, active presence in the world. The teaching ministry of the church is never simply a human activity because it involves both God's initiative and God's empowerment. The power of the Holy Spirit at work in the church energizes it to the end that it can be a teaching community.

*respond in faith and love,*

While the initiative remains with God, there is a moment that calls for a personal response. That response is the act of accepting in faith and love what has been freely offered of God's gracious and redeeming love. The marvel of God's grace is that it never compels.

*that as new persons in Christ*

The result of faith to God's invitation is the creation of the new person. The transformation is so total and so life-changing that only the analogy of birth is adequate to describe it. The objective of the teaching church is to have an ever-growing community of new creations in Christ.

*they may know who they are and what their human situation means,*

The new person in Christ must discover what the commitment means in terms of very specific human situations. The new life does not come equipped with all the answers. The issues of values, meanings, and priorities persist throughout life. The church, or the teaching community, is the arena in which persons can explore together the basic life questions.

*grow as children of God*

Growth is the expected outcome of new life. In the community of faith that growth takes many forms. Individuals remain unique creations and together they reflect a marvelous variety of individual differences. A very significant dimension of growth is the relational one. Persons in the Christian community grow closer to God and one another. They never attain full intimacy, but they move toward an ideal, sharing a sense of fulfillment as they grow.

*rooted in the Christian community,*

The importance of community in the process of nurture and development can never be overemphasized. Persons cannot grow apart from the necessary support of and interaction with others. Persons who are not rooted in the community of faith are cut off from the necessary resources for survival. It is through participation in and identification with the teaching community that one is nurtured in the faith.

*live in obedience to the will of God in every relationship,*

The rule of life for the community of new persons in Christ is obedience to the will of God. Every relationship and human situation comes under the authority of this rule. Life is no longer divided into neat compartments where the religious dimension is carefully controlled and limited. One of the tasks of the teaching church is to struggle to discover the full meaning of God's will and its implications for living.

*fulfill their common vocation in the world,*

Those who follow Christ may have avocations, but they share the common calling to be the reconciling presence of Christ in the world. They are commissioned to bring healing to a world of brokenness. Equipping persons for such a ministry is an unending task.

*and abide in the Christian hope.*

The climax of the goal of the teaching church is the affirmation of hope. In an uncertain and unpredictable world, the community of faith finds its unfailing support and its unchanging certainty in the love and grace of the One who was, who is, and who is to be. The community of faith knows in whom it has believed and rests secure in the knowledge that God who creates and redeems will always sustain it.

## Functions of the Teaching Church[1]

When a church begins to think of itself as a teaching church, it has an organizing principle around which it can build its educational ministry. There are at least five basic functions which must be carried out if a church is to fulfill its teaching ministry.

Function: *To affirm the foundations of its teaching ministry.*

[1]This section is taken from "Understanding the Concept of a Teaching Church," by Grant Hanson, chapter 1 in *The Teaching Church at Work,* ed. Kenneth D. Blazier (Valley Forge: Judson Press, 1980), pp. 10-11.

A teaching church begins with the biblical revelation and the Christian heritage. As it assimilates these biblical, theological, and historical perspectives, its teaching is made relevant and significant when it brings the light of the gospel to bear upon the life issues of today. Without adequate biblical and theological rootage the teaching ministry can never fulfill its basic commission. The safeguard against perversion or error is an adequate grounding in the tenets of the historic faith.

An understanding and appreciation of the continuing work of the Holy Spirit in the ministry of teaching are necessary parts of the foundation. Christian teaching is always more than a human enterprise. It is a sacred responsibility that has about it a dimension of mystery and wonder.

The foundations of the teaching ministry also include an understanding of the nature of growing persons. Effective teaching always takes into account the persons who are being taught. An awareness of the many ways persons grow sharpens sensitivity to the uniqueness of every human being.

The learning process itself is also an important aspect of the foundations for teaching. To understand how persons learn is basic to a meaningful teaching ministry.

Function: *To plan for the most effective teaching ministry.*

Planning is the key to an effective teaching ministry. A teaching church establishes its goals and the plans for their accomplishment. Goals that are significant emerge out of the awareness of the needs of persons in light of the gospel. Each church accepts the responsibility for defining its specific goals based on the perceptions of its particular situation.

Organizational structures are necessary to carry the responsibility for planning and administering a program. A duly constituted board or committee charged with overseeing the total educational program will tend to foster coordination and comprehensiveness.

One essential element in successful program development is the involvement and support of the congregation. A teaching church cannot fulfill its ministry unless the whole congregation is involved. Good planning makes provision for giving the congregation a sense of "ownership." Without ownership the level of commitment on the part of the members is minimal.

Function: *To develop leaders for a variety of ministries.*

A teaching church cannot function without a corps of leaders prepared to fulfill a variety of ministries. These leaders must be recruited, motivated, trained, assigned, and supported. Their development includes personal growth, understanding of the learning processes, sensitivity to the needs of persons, and acquisition of basic skills. The quality of the program is largely dependent on the quality of leadership. Because the need for new leaders is constant, the plan of enlistment, training, and support must be ongoing.

A teaching church is concerned, furthermore, not only with the designated leaders but also with the broader responsibility of "equipping persons for ministry." Everyone in the community of faith has gifts, recognized or unrecognized. If the gifts are unrecognized, they need to be discovered. An aspect of the Christian growth of every person is the development of the capacity to exercise leadership in one form or another.

Function: *To nurture persons in Christian growth.*

A teaching church is a nurturing community. Its goal is to provide a loving and caring environment in which persons can grow in the Christian faith and experience. It recognizes that the Christian life is a maturing process with many stages of development from infancy to adulthood. Persons within a single congregation reflect many degrees of progress toward the objective of maturity. There is a beautiful blend of naiveté and sophistication, ignorance and wisdom, inexperience and experience. All are learners and all are teachers. The interaction and interrelationship across the total life cycle enrich the experience of all.

Growing persons are helped most when there has been intentional planning. It is important that the church set out deliberately to provide learning experiences for persons of all ages, in which they can come to understand themselves and their experiences in the light of the gospel. A church needs to design an educational program which in systematic fashion seeks to support the growth process.

The quality of life of the congregation is a vital factor in effective nurture. Much learning is unplanned and unintentional. When there is inconsistency between what the congregation professes and what it practices, negative learning is a real possibility. A teaching church needs to remember that it is called above all else to be a redemptive community which gives and supports life.

Function: *To enable the fulfillment of the church's mission in the world.*

A teaching church recognizes that it always exists in relation to the world. Its ministry attempts to bridge the gap between the gospel and the world. It is concerned with fostering the intersection of the Christian faith with life.

A part of growing as an individual Christian is the development of a sense of vocation. Involvement in mission is the normal expectation for all who seek to live as disciples of Jesus Christ.

It is important, moreover, that a teaching church express its involvement in mission corporately. God's calling is to the church collectively as well as individually. The church involved in a community ministry is fulfilling its teaching role in a most telling way.

Together these five functions provide the conceptual framework upon which a church can build its ministry of teaching. These functions help to answer the question about the scope of the task faced by a church that wants to take its responsibility seriously.

## Foundations for a Teaching Church

Against the background of the concept of the teaching church as it has been described, the task at hand now is to develop an understanding of those foundational components that underlie and support the nature and ministry of the teaching church. None of the foundational components stands in isolation, but for purposes of study it is helpful to examine each one separately. The following chapters attempt to describe the foundations that a church will want to affirm as it seeks to be faithful to its commission to be a teaching community.

# 2

# Jesus Christ: The Foundation

"For no other foundation can any one lay than that which is laid, which is Jesus Christ" (1 Corinthians 3:11).

The heart of the teaching ministry of the church is the person and work of Jesus Christ. Any system that describes itself as Christian has to begin at this point. Paul said it very clearly when he declared that "no other foundation can any one lay. . . ." In Ephesians 2:20 Christ is called "the cornerstone." The faith system of the church begins with and revolves around Jesus Christ.

The basic question to be asked of one coming into the Christian community is: "Do you promise to follow Jesus Christ as Lord and Savior?" The assumption is that one will not necessarily understand all that that commitment means, but one does have to understand that this promise is the starting point. The call to discipleship is the call to a growing and maturing relationship between the disciple and the Master. The community that is built upon these relationships is, in the language of the New Testament, the "body of Christ." It is the expression of his living and continuing presence in the world.

The ultimate revelation of God comes in Christ. He is the Word that comes from God. He is the embodiment of the Good News sent from God. All that has been revealed of God is seen in Jesus Christ. In Christ the world is being reconciled to God. The teaching ministry of the church starts at the point of affirming this one supreme reality, that "the Word became flesh and dwelt among us, full of grace and truth; we have beheld his glory, glory as of the only Son from the Father" (John 1:14).

## The Bold Claim

The claim which the early church made was that Jesus is Lord. He is the Christ, the Messiah, the Anointed One. For the first followers, who were Jews, it was a great leap of faith to declare that the one whom they followed was the Messiah. The early baptismal formula was simply "I believe that Jesus is the Messiah." (There was much misunderstanding about the nature of that messiahship, even among the twelve who were closest to Jesus. The common expectation was that the Messiah would bring deliverance from oppression and usher in a new age. Jesus had to work constantly to try to help his followers understand that his mission was not simply to throw off the yoke of Roman oppression. Even toward the close of his public ministry, as Jesus anticipated going to Jerusalem, Peter rebuked him for talking about suffering and dying at the hands of the authorities in Jerusalem.)

It is not easy for us to appreciate the risk that persons took when they acknowledged Jesus as Messiah. They were not simply making the claim that he was a good man, a wise teacher, or an able prophet, but, rather, they were claiming that he was God's Chosen One, prophesied of old. He was the very Word of God existing from the beginning with God. No one died for saying that Jesus was a good man, but untold numbers suffered and died for the claim that this same Jesus was both Lord and Christ. The claim that the first Christians made was a tremendous one upon which they literally staked their lives. They were so bold as to declare that at this point (the first century) and place (Palestine) in history God came into the world in the person of Jesus Christ. That affirmation continues to be the core of all that the church seeks to teach.

All history has been affected by the event of God in Christ entering the human scene. This impact is part of the message that the church has to bring to the world. The claim that the church makes for Jesus Christ is still bold and audacious. It declares that God is still at work in the world through the church. The body of Christ witnesses to the living presence of Christ in the world. The work of reconciliation is not complete. The mission of the church is to be the faithful witness to the reconciling power of God's love and peace as they have been manifest in Jesus Christ. This message of reconciliation is the foundation upon which the teaching ministry is built.

The expressions of the Christian faith have taken many forms. There are varieties of understandings about the nature of discipleship. Theologies emphasize many different concerns. The differences seem very important, giving the impression of endless diversity. While diversity exists, the supreme fact remains that the whole community of faith affirms that Jesus Christ is Lord. All are made one in the commitment to him as Savior and Lord. The history of the church makes it clear that statements of theology are shaped by the times and situations. The changes in theology come in order that the work and person of Jesus Christ remain the central focus of the faith. Because the presence of Christ is alive in the church, the church is able to lift up a witness that is ever new and relevant to the setting in which that witness is being declared. Everything can and does change except the central focus, which is Christ.

## The Model for Ministry

The person and work of Jesus are foundational for the church because they provide the models for the ministry of the church. The teaching church models the ministry of its Lord. The brief years of Jesus' public ministry were committed primarily to teaching. The common designation for him was "teacher." His relationship to the Twelve was that of a teacher. They were disciples or learners who were being prepared to carry on his work once the years of his public ministry were completed.

The model of Jesus as teacher is critical for the church in the development of the style of its own teaching ministry. With Jesus, teaching was never limited to the formal or structured situation. He used whatever occasion presented itself as an opportunity for teaching. His curriculum was all of life, and the disciples learned to expect the unexpected teaching. Likewise, the church must always remember that it teaches not only in the formal and structured situation but also in all of the daily relationships and interactions it has with persons.

One of the obvious characteristics of Jesus as a teacher was his superb sensitivity to persons. In a day when women and children were frequently shunted to the side, he dealt with them as though they counted. Such unusual behavior for a teacher of that time occasioned both comments and criticisms, even from those closest to him. He was interested in those whom polite society chose to exclude. He went as a guest to the house of Zacchaeus, a despised tax collector, and helped him to discover the potential that God had given him. The woman condemned as an adultress was befriended by Jesus and given the exciting possibility of a new life. He saw not what persons were but always what they might become.

One of the marvelous aspects of Jesus' relationship to people was his willingness to take time with them. For example, he had time for children even though the disciples grew impatient with him. He recognized the importance of children and saw the potential within them. For Jesus, persons came first.

The teaching church reflects faithfulness to the Lord's example when it remembers that its ministry is with people. Those people cannot be limited only to those upon whom "polite" society places its stamp of approval. They must include persons of all ages and backgrounds. Other concerns must never preempt the church's vital focus upon ministry with persons. The leader who ignores or brushes aside the child is not following the example of Jesus. It takes time to deal with individuals. It means that schedules cannot always be kept. A church reveals much about itself by the ways it deals with the young, the elderly, the handicapped, the dispossessed, and the outcast. A genuine love for persons is the evidence that the church has understood Jesus' example.

Another characteristic of Jesus' teaching ministry was the capacity to relate faith to everyday life. Jesus did not talk about propositions of faith but about things with which people were familiar in day-to-day living. He understood the economic, social, and political realities of the times, and he chose to use the situations and circumstances of ordinary people as the framework for presenting the issues of faith. His language, while eloquent, was strikingly simple and down to earth. He avoided the language of the religious "insiders" who loved to talk among themselves but were incomprehensible to the uninitiated. His concern was that persons have understanding, not that he impress someone with his erudition. Those who heard him went away saying that they had never heard a teacher like him. The crowds came because he spoke to them in terms that they understood and used illustrations from everyday living. Jesus never told them just what they wanted to hear. Occasionally he disturbed them greatly, for he spoke fearlessly on touchy issues. When necessary he was confrontational, to the point that he generated hostility and opposition. It was always clear what he was attempting to teach.

The church is called to deliver its message in simple and understandable terms. Unfortunately, such communication guidelines are not always followed. More than they may realize, persons within the church speak in "insider's" language that is foreign to many persons outside the church. The church must never assume that simply because it has spoken words, there has been communication. Rather, it should always follow the example of its Lord who, when he adressed the crowds, began where they were and used language familiar to them.

Another primary characteristic of the ministry of Jesus was his concern for the ultimate issues of human existence. Whenever he met an individual and engaged him or her in conversation, he got immediately to those ultimate issues. A primary focus of his teaching was the concept of the kingdom of God, i.e., the rule of God in the hearts and lives of people. The kingdom is a present reality which becomes operative whenever persons order their lives after the will of God. Jesus' teaching described the principles that should be followed in all the relationships of life. The disciples did not understand these principles because they continued to look for a king who would overthrow the tyranny of Rome and usher in a new age of political independence. Their preconceptions of the kingdom of God made it difficult to grasp Jesus' teaching when he talked about humility, meekness, righteousness, mercy, purity of heart, peace, forgiveness, endurance of persecution, and the love of enemies. These qualities would be expressed in the person seeking to live in faithfulness under the will of God. Jesus dealt with these issues when he encountered people. He cut right to the core and confronted individuals with the basic issues of their relationships toward God and one another.

The church easily becomes engrossed in a multitude of concerns and is frequently distracted by a variety of demands for its time and attention. There are many worthy causes in which the church can invest resources and energy. If it is faithful to the Lord, however, it will stop to take stock and be reminded of the single-mindedness with which Jesus ordered his priorities. The teaching church keeps its ministry focused on the primary task to which it is called. It reminds itself that its model is always Jesus, whom his contemporaries called "teacher."

## The Commission

The teaching church has more than the model of Jesus as its directive. It has the very express commission given to the early church: "Go therefore and make disciples of all nations . . . teaching them . . ." (Matthew 28:19-20). The Great Commission, as it is known, is readily identifiable with evangelism and the task of the church to share the Good News with persons to the ends of the earth. It is clear, however, that it is also an imperative to teach. Persons are to be made learners, which is the literal meaning of "disciple." The command is to share the Good News and to undertake the process of discipling.

A tension has sometimes been developed between evangelism and education by putting one in opposition with the other or emphasizing one to the exclusion of the other. Such tension is not consistent with the Commission, which recognizes no such division between the two. The teaching church recognizes its calling to share the Good News with persons everywhere as well as its role in making disciples.

Teaching is an imperative for the church, but it has not always been made a priority. The early church took its teaching mandate with great seriousness. Perhaps the synagogue tradition carried over the importance of teaching. New converts were given careful instruction before they were allowed full standing in the fellowship. As the centuries passed, the teaching ministry of the church in the formal sense became haphazard. Instruction of the laity was increasingly equated with a limited catechetical instruction with emphasis on rote memory. The church was dominated by the clergy, and the laity was excluded from leadership. It is not surprising that the Sunday school movement, which arose in the latter part of the eighteenth century, was inspired and directed by the laity. For all its limitations, the Sunday school expressed a deep underlying concern on the part of large numbers of persons for a teaching ministry in the church that had long been neglected. The struggle continues because the church still tends to make its teaching program peripheral. It is frequently identified with children, with little attention given to youth and adults. The clearest evidence of the problem is the identification of "church" with what happens in the sanctuary on Sunday morning. Other activities and programs may be fine, but they are not thought of as "church." Unconsciously and perhaps unintentionally, the ministry of teaching is relegated to a position of lesser importance alongside the "real" work of the church.

The teaching church comes back to affirm again and again that it is directed by the explicit command of the Lord to make teaching a top priority. It never loses sight of the fact that its primary job is to make disciples of girls and boys and women and men. It constantly reminds itself that it has the mandate to teach. Obedience to the Lord leaves the teaching church with no other alternative.

# 3

# The Biblical Foundation

The written Word is foundational to the life and ministry of the teaching church. Christians are sometimes described as "people of the Book," and in truth they are. The Scriptures are the unique record of God's self-disclosure in creation, in history, and in Jesus Christ. The basic guide for the church in its life and mission is always the Bible. It gives the church the message to be carried to persons everywhere. It represents the common heritage shared by all who profess Christ as Savior and Lord.

As the church grounds itself in the testimony of Scripture, its mind and heart are opened to the truth of God. Understanding is deepened and developed, and faith is nurtured and matured. The community of faith is the proper place for the written Word to be received and understood. In a sense, only the church can teach the Bible, because interpretation and understanding cannot be separated from the past and ongoing faith experience of the church.

The story of the Bible helps the church to understand its place in God's whole redemptive plan for humankind. This story never ceases to amaze those who probe its depths. It begins as a love story between the creator God and an insignificant little family band on the eastern edge of the Mediterranean Sea. The family does not represent the power or prestige of any ancient empire. Its only distinguishing quality is a stubborn belief in one God. The people stumble and falter many times, but the thread of faithfulness is never lost, even though it is maintained only by a handful of the faithful. The relationship comes to be expressed in terms of a covenant. Part of the marvel of the story is how that covenantal relationship, which was interpreted originally in exclusive terms, gradually broadens to encompass all persons everywhere. God's special love and favor are not for one small family only, but for the whole world.

When the early church started to develop the canon of the Scriptures, the story began with Judaism's account of the creation and God's self-disclosure and climaxed with the Revelation account of a new heaven and a new earth. The story is a great drama, catching all God's redemptive activity in the past, present, and future. It sets the purpose and meaning of human existence in cosmic terms linking it to God's own purpose. Once the church understands its own place in this awesome drama, its mission becomes apparent.

## The Problem Book

Though all agree that the Bible is the church's book, its guide for faith and practice, a problem begins at this point of agreement. The Bible is an extremely difficult book to understand and interpret. It both unites and divides the church. The pages of history recount the bitter struggles over the variations of interpretation among persons who counted themselves among the community of faith. Wars have been fought over conflicting understandings of the Scriptures. Christians have refused to recognize other Christians because their interpretations of the Bible seemed to be irreconcilable. When the church sets out to teach from the Bible, it assumes an arduous and demanding task.

To begin with, the Bible is a collection of books written by many different authors in many different places over many years. The period from the earliest to the latest writings stretches over a thousand years. The writings include a variety of literary forms: historical narrative, poetry, songs, laws, oracles, wise sayings, short stories, letters, and apocalypses. The forms reflect the particular times in which the material was written as well as the specific content. Some of the literary forms are strange and unfamiliar to the average reader. One of the difficulties people have in using the Bible is that it has this amazing scope and variety of material. The serious student of the Bible takes great care to understand the uniqueness and particular characteristics of each specific portion of the Scriptures.

Another problem for the modern reader emerges from the fact that the writings of the Bible are ancient. While it is true that the relevance of the writings for our own times and situations is sometimes astounding, we must always remember that the material had its setting in real-life situations a very long time ago. There may be great similarities between problems we are facing and those described in the text, but it is important to remember that the problems addressed are those of that ancient time, not today. When Paul dealt with the problems of the churches in the first century, he was dealing with the issues of that moment, not of the twentieth century. He was not thinking about what his messages to the churches were going to mean to persons living centuries later. It is amazing to realize how much of what he wrote is applicable to the life of the church today, but that is very different from saying that he was writing for us today. The Scriptures are misused when they are made to speak as though they were addressed to a contemporary situation. This in no way denies the fact that history produces many parallels and that ancient truth can have application to a modern issue.

The materials of the Bible are ancient and none of the original manuscripts still exist. The original parchments were perishable and disintegrated long ago. What exist today are copies of copies of copies of copies. There are perhaps five thousand Greek manuscripts of the New Testament of varying ages and in various states of condition. A much more limited number of Old Testament manuscripts of varying condition still exist. The task of the biblical scholars is to study all these manuscripts, make comparisons, analyze the variations, and then compose the most accurate and authentic text possible. The task never ends, and periodically new manuscript materials are discovered, such as those discovered from the Qumran community (the Dead Sea Scrolls). The great variety of translations and revisions simply serves to illustrate that the process of producing the best biblical text for contemporary readers is never finished.

The world of the Bible is not only ancient but alien as well. The biblical culture differs in many respects from modern Western culture. To move from an industrialized, urbanized, scientific way of life back to a more crude and ancient culture requires a genuine understanding of and appreciation for the nature and values of that ancient culture.

Family relationships were of great importance in the biblical world. (The Old Testament is basically the story of a family.) Family ties were extremely strong, and maintaining family integrity was paramount. The history of the people was a family-centered history, which explains the great preoccupation with genealogies. The individual had great responsibilities to the family which were expected to be fulfilled at all costs. The individual represented the family and therefore conducted herself or himself in ways that reflected honor on the family. Life was tightly controlled by the family mores and traditions. The identity of the individual was subordinated to the identity of the group. Society was tribal, with family groups linked together for mutual support.

The society was also nomadic, with family groups (tribes) moving with their flocks to fresh grazing lands. City dwellers were the exception rather than the rule of the Old Testament life. The nomadic life was expressed in biblical symbols and language. The image of the shepherd in both Old and New Testaments illustrates how deeply ingrained in people's understanding was the life of the nomad and the flocks. The most appropriate image for God had to be shepherd, because the good shepherd fed and cared for the flock. The modern reader can grasp the imagery of the nomad and the flock, but the imagery is not a part of his or her day-by-day experience. The practice of selecting animals from the flock for a sacrifice is also something outside the experience of the contemporary reader.

The ancient people had a love for words and sounds. Long before written language had emerged, these people developed their stories, wise sayings, and poems. They were great observers of life and the world around them. They liked to describe their reflections in different literary forms which were told and retold. In the retelling were refinements and improvements that polished the stories more and more. The storytellers would discover a certain play on words or a pleasant sound that would increase the listeners' enjoyment and ability to retain the material. Insights and wisdom were refined by this process of oral tradition until they were written down to be preserved for future generations. To a modern scientific age this long and somewhat tedious process for distilling and preserving human wisdom is strange and without parallel.

Biblical language tends to be much more vivid and imaginative than contemporary language. The writers had great skill in communicating word pictures. They preferred images to descriptions. When biblical language is treated as scientific or analytical, great violence can be done to the meaning of the text. The Bible abounds in symbolism, metaphors, similes, and hyperboles. Metaphors use a word or phrase to suggest a likeness or analogy between two objects or ideas. It is quite impossible to understand the Bible without appreciating its endless use of metaphors. God is king, shepherd, light, salvation, rock, and fortress, to suggest only a few. Among the images of Jesus are son, lamb, shepherd, foundation, new Adam, way, truth, life. Some images used for Christians are light, salt, saints, people of God, and royal priesthood. All of these images are extremely helpful and insightful, but care must be taken not to treat them as literal.

The hyperbole becomes a troublesome literary form when one attempts to deal with it literally. The very exaggeration of the statement drives home the truth being emphasized. The statement about the camel and the eye of the needle is not to be explained away by trying to think that somehow a camel could go through the eye of a needle by identifying the eye as some kind of gate or opening. The point is that it is unbelievably difficult for a rich man to enter the kingdom of heaven. The hyperbole does not rule out the possibility that a rich man could get into heaven; rather, it drives home the point that riches are a great obstacle to entrance into the kingdom. The hyperbole is very powerful because it imprints an image on the consciousness that is not soon forgotten. The exaggeration of the image is what makes it so effective.

Biblical language is rich in symbolism that, when taken literally, is confusing and misleading. Symbols used in apocalyptic writings like Daniel and Revelation communicated clearly to persons in a particular situation. Apocalyptic writing has a very specific context, such as the persecution the Jews of the second century B.C. were suffering under Antiochus Epiphanes (which was the setting for the Book of Daniel). Such writing does not prophesy current events but delivers a message of encouragement and hope to those being persecuted. The meaning of the message is hidden to the outsider, thus protecting both the writer and the readers. The task of the modern reader is to uncover the meaning of the symbolism in the setting that it was used, and not to distort the symbolism by attempting to place it in a modern context. The fact has to be accepted that some of the symbolism of the writing remains a mystery because not enough is known about particular situations to which the writing was addressed.

The issue for biblical interpretation is to maintain faithfulness to the relation of the ancient text and its situation while seeking to discover the meanings and truths for life today. Obviously the Bible teaches us about the ancient world, and in that sense it is like any other literature from ancient times. Classified among the world's great literature, the Bible can be and is studied as such. What true biblical interpretation seeks, however, is the marvelous revelation of God, which can bring men and women of every nation to a redemptive relationship with the God of our Lord Jesus Christ. The intent of all study and interpretation is to come to the awareness of God's full purpose for humanity. At that point variations of interpretation and differences of understanding pale.

The Bible recounts the mighty acts of God through which persons come into a life-transforming relationship with the living God. This is all that the teaching church needs.

## Guides for Interpreting Scripture[1]

If persons are totally free to interpret for themselves without guidelines, the possibility for the distortion of Scripture becomes very great. The church has found it necessary to agree upon some basic rules that help individual interpreters remain faithful to the true nature of the writings. The rules are quite simple, but they are essential to the ministry of the teaching church.

First, the Scriptures must be approached with an open mind so that the truth can be experienced as it is revealed. Amazingly, some persons are primarily interested in using the Bible as a tool to reinforce their own positions. They have already determined the truth and turn to the Bible to lend authority to their version of the truth. Such an approach brings little understanding or insight. Using the Bible to bolster an argument may be a legitimate tactic for a debate, but it is a poor way to discover new truth. The searching mind, by contrast, has the excitement and anticipation that a new measure of God's truth will reward patient and diligent study. What awaits discovery by the open, receptive mind and heart can never be predicted.

Second, biblical passages need to be interpreted in light of their literary form. Prose can be matter of fact and literal. Poetry, on the other hand, is highly imaginative and emotional. It uses metaphors and symbols to reach the feelings as well as the intellect. Hebrew poetry is filled with vivid images and repeated parallelisms. It plays on words and sounds. Poetry needs to be read aloud so that the ear as well as the eye can share the experience. Because more than one-third of the Old Testament is poetry, it is important to recognize the basic difference between prose and poetry.

Other literary forms also have specific characteristics. The Gospels are not true biographies but testimonials of persons who knew Jesus. Their purpose is to persuade readers of the truth about the claims of Jesus Christ and to evoke the response of faith. They are interpreted history rather than a simple recording of facts.

The letters of the New Testament were written to specific groups of persons in very specific circumstances. The letters addressed particular

[1] See Edward P. Blair, *The Bible and You* (Nashville: Abingdon Press, 1953), chapter 2. Blair's book is the basis of this section.

historical situations and were not primarily designed to declare universal truth. The fact that they seem to have relevance for the life of the churches today does not obviate the fact that they were written as counsel to specific groups of people in specific situations. This means that the teaching may or may not be relevant in today's church.

Additional comments could be made about other types of material found in the Bible. It is sufficient to say that the integrity of each literary form must be respected if one is to develop a correct interpretation of and appreciation for the material being studied.

Third, it is important to try to discover the meaning of the words when they were first written and first read. Words change with the passage of time. The trouble some people have understanding certain words and expressions in the King James Version illustrates the changes in the English language that have occurred in less than four hundred years. This example can only suggest the problem of dealing with ancient language explaining situations that occurred more than two thousand years ago. Modern readers must exercise great caution in reading ancient materials so as not to impose their own meanings and understandings on those materials. Words are symbols that groups of persons give agreed-upon meanings. It is dangerous to assume that present-day meanings are the meanings those words had many centuries ago. Language arises out of life and is constantly changing and developing. The concern of biblical translators is to recover the meanings of passages as they were written and read in their original settings. The effort to find those meanings has led to the development of many paraphrases of Scripture. These paraphrases are not literal translations and, in fact, sometimes take great liberties with the biblical text. They can be extremely helpful in the search for the meaning of a passage in today's language, but caution must be exercised—remember, they are paraphrases, not translations. A wise procedure is always to check the paraphrase against a standard translation and even against other paraphrases.

This step of seeking to discover a passage's original meaning is easily overlooked because often the concern for determining what a passage means in the contemporary scene takes priority. The fact remains, however, that sound biblical study always first asks "What was the author trying to say? What did this passage mean to those who first read or heard it?" By neglecting to answer those questions, persons can misunderstand or misinterpret the true meaning of a passage.

Fourth, biblical passages always need to be interpreted in context.

Serious error of biblical interpretation is to lift words or phrases out of their contexts. In truth, the Bible can be made to support almost any position by carefully selecting excerpts that seem to prove the point while ignoring the context of those excerpts.

The practice of slavery has been justified on biblical grounds at various times in history. It is possible to find passages that speak of slavery and can be made to build a case for the institution of slavery. The fact that some of these passages were merely describing situations in which slavery did exist does not justify their use to advocate the practice. An issue such as slavery has to be viewed from the whole perspective of the Bible, which obviously never advocates the institution of slavery. Violence is done to Scripture when passages are used or interpreted in ways that contradict or deny the basic message of the whole Bible.

Whenever the words "the Bible says" are heard, it is important to check that what is cited is, in truth, what the Bible says. An appeal to biblical authority for support of a matter is perfectly legitimate, provided that the passage is not used simply to support a position without regard to its context and the context of the whole message of the Scriptures. The rule is to allow the Bible to say what it has to say in the light of the whole biblical revelation.

Fifth, a sound practice in the study of the Bible is to stick with the simplest or most natural interpretation of a passage. Some persons are intrigued with the thought of secret or double meanings. They are excited with the prospect of hidden meanings that are revealed only to a chosen few. Such delight is an ancient "practice" dating back to early centuries of the church. The results of these intrigues frequently have produced some extremely bizarre interpretations of Scripture. Hence, the best rule is to accept the words of Scripture as they are written, with the message they communicate.

Portions of Scripture considered apocalyptic include the books of Daniel and Revelation. The writings are highly symbolic and filled with vivid imagery. They cannot be read literally because they are communicating a hidden message. The important thing to keep in mind is that these materials came out of times of persecution. They were messages of hope and encouragement meant to sustain the community of faith in troubling times. They had a very specific historical context and dealt with particular problems and issues of that time. The message was veiled to the outsider, but it spoke clearly to the people of faith. The problem for the contemporary reader is to get back to the original message as understood by the church rather than interpret the material to fit modern situations. To twist the interpretation of a certain passage, to make it appear relevant to a present-day issue, is an abuse of the biblical materials.

The wisest practice is to treat passages as meaning what they say and avoid the temptation to treat them allegorically. The Bible was written to *communicate* both truth and understanding, not to veil them.

Sixth, the message of the Bible needs always to be treated holistically. It is true that the message has many parts and a variety of forms, but they all fit together. From beginning to end the theme of the Bible is God's creative and redemptive activity in relation to humanity. The Bible is sometimes described as the story of the mighty acts of God, an unfolding drama that sweeps across the centuries. It is important to remember that the story is understood in the light of divine revelation in the life, death, and resurrection of Jesus Christ. The Bible is the book of the church, and the church reads it from the special perspective it receives from the life and ministry of the Lord.

The importance of trying to understand the parts of the Bible in terms of the whole cannot be overemphasized. A holistic approach acts as a safeguard against the reduction of certain passages or themes to proof texts. It provides a framework for dealing with problem areas and apparent contradictions. Such an approach serves as a guide to the development of interpretations with integrity. The full grandeur of the biblical story can be experienced only when one exposes himself or herself to the whole sweep of the message.

The church takes seriously its use of the Scriptures. The principles of biblical interpretation have evolved out of long years of experience. The rules are simple, and their only purpose is that the integrity of the Scriptures be maintained and proper interpretation be encouraged.

## Message of the Bible for Today

The most abiding elements in human history are the fundamental experiences of the human spirit. Everything else in life changes; outwardly our environments and inwardly our mental states are altered. However, at the very core of our beings is something that changes very little if at all. The motives that cause us to act have varied very little through history.

There must be a distinction between enduring experiences and their temporary expressions. We no longer put on sackcloth and ashes, but that does not mean that any important change has taken place in the griefs and miseries that sackcloth and ashes once expressed.

The fast-changing nature of this modern world gives a sense of impermanence to life, but not to be forgotten is that in addition to this modern world is a sphere of human experience that is not new at all but as old as the race: sin and its consequence, hunger and thirst after righteousness, love, hate, jealousy, heartbreak, grief and tragedy, joy, hope, and the need for God. The Bible enables us to step out of the shifting, changing world into the depths of the human spirit where the enduring experiences dwell. In the world where real-life issues are faced, what is new?

Are selfishness, lust, friendship, self-sacrifice, remorse, pardon, and reconciliation new? Are the desires for peace, freedom, or justice new? The strength of the Bible has always been its appeal to the deep and abiding realm of basic human experience.

The Bible is foundational to the teaching church because it brings a message that is relevant to the needs of the human situation. The task of the church is to let the divine spirit lead it to discover fresh meaning and a deepened knowledge of the content of this written Word.

# 4

# The Continuing Work of the Holy Spirit

"But the Counselor, the Holy Spirit, whom the Father will send in my name, he will teach you all things, and bring to your remembrance all that I have said to you" (John 14:26). As Jesus described the coming of the Holy Spirit to the disciples, he made it clear that his teaching ministry would continue. The teaching he did with the Twelve would be carried on to preserve and to reinforce all that he had shared with them.

One of the foundations of the ministry of the teaching church is the affirmation that the Holy Spirit is present and at work. God has not left the church alone with only its own resources. The presence of the living Spirit guarantees that the church can continue to work with power and effectiveness. As always, the initiative and the energy for ministry come from the Lord, who is Spirit.

Jesus promised his followers that they would have power when the Holy Spirit came upon them and that they would be witnesses to him, beginning near at hand and going to the ends of the earth. The story of the early church is the story of how that transforming power was manifest in the lives of persons. People could see power that expressed itself in new moral resources and quality of life. The sheer power of the Spirit in the lives of those early Christians became a force that drew men and women to Christ. Paul put it this way: "For our gospel came to you not only in word, but also in power and in the Holy Spirit and with full conviction" (1 Thessalonians 1:5).

This is the tradition in which the church finds itself today as it seeks to be faithful to its Lord to be the community that faithfully teaches.

It is the successor of that early church which moved out into the world with new authority and effectiveness. It is important again to affirm that the teaching church is energized by the Spirit of the living God.

## The Plus in Christian Teaching

The church must always have the goal to provide the finest possible teaching-learning experience that it can offer. Its responsibility is to see that its educational program maintains the highest standards of quality. Otherwise, it might appear that the church has not taken its commission seriously. It has to recognize that there is much to be learned from educational programs other than its own.

*Good planning* is basic. Effective teaching-learning can never emerge from a hit-or-miss approach. Clear goals and specific objectives provide the framework upon which the program can be built. Planning also deals with the means to achieve the desired outcome.

The *selection and training of good leadership* is another key to effective education. The quality of any educational program largely is a reflection of the quality of its leadership. This is even more true for teaching in the church, where much of the learning grows out of the sharing of the faith experience between the mature and the less mature.

*Well-designed teaching resources* make their contribution to an effective education process. Though only tools, they give purpose and direction as well as specific helps to the teacher in designing a course or a series of lessons. The plan for learning they provide takes into account past experiences and anticipates future ones. Curriculum assures that the goals are kept in focus and the planned outcomes are realized.

One of the very important elements in a good educational program is the *learning environment*. Attractive surroundings invite persons to come and to participate. Comfort and safety are part of a positive atmosphere. The church has to remember that it communicates to persons by the surroundings that it provides. Far more significant than the mere physical environment will be the "feeling tone" that people will perceive. The most attractive physical facilities are incidental to an atmosphere of interest, concern, caring, and love expressed toward people. The message needs to be unmistakably clear that people are important and that each individual counts.

All these elements contribute significantly to the establishment of a good teaching-learning program. The church has much to learn—and it has learned—from other educational institutions. It is fair to say that good education is good education be it inside or outside the church.

The church ought never dare to allow its standards or its expectations to be lower than those of other teaching groups. The teaching ministry of the church is too important to accept less than the best standards.

The implication of what has been said about education in the church is that it is in many ways similar to education in other places. There is a measure of truth in this, but the differences are tremendously significant. More than subject matter is different, although obviously the church deals with a unique and very special body of material related to its faith experience. The transmission of this material is secondary to the nurturing process that seeks to develop mature disciples committed to Jesus Christ as Savior and Lord.

That which ultimately distinguishes teaching in the church from teaching in other places is the astounding claim that God is involved in the teaching-learning process in a way that goes far beyond human enterprise. The Holy Spirit is the power that makes the teaching of the church life-transforming. This does not relieve the church of the responsibility to give of the best of its resources to its teaching ministry, but beyond the best efforts that faithful men and women can bring is this somewhat incomprehensible participation of the Spirit of the living God.

The audacity of this claim becomes more apparent as one draws a mental picture of a rather typical teaching situation in many congregations. The church is small and has a constant struggle to find leadership. A young woman has been recruited as the teacher of a class of older elementary boys and girls. She has had little training and virtually no experience. The church does provide her with teaching materials, which she uses as best she can to prepare for the session. On Sunday morning she is confronted with seven or eight wiggly, easily distracted children. She struggles doggedly to make it a helpful learning experience, but the outcome does not appear to be too hopeful. This glimpse of the church attempting to fulfill its teaching ministry may be more typical than we care to admit. Yet this is not the total picture because in the midst of this somewhat unpromising situation God is at work in the life of that teacher and in the lives of those boys and girls. Some of the sessions will appear to be disasters and the teacher will grow discouraged, but as the weeks and months pass, learning does take place. The teacher herself grows in faith and understanding. The boys and girls grow, and their changes in attitude, behavior, and belief become apparent. The teacher makes the amazing discovery that not everything depends upon her and that the Spirit of God is at work in the teaching process. In spite of her own inadequacies and limitations, significant changes and growth take place in that classroom. Just how the Spirit works in the church's ministry of teaching remains a mystery. It is beyond our capacity to understand or explain, but we bear witness to the lives that are changed. The teaching church has power infinitely beyond its own resources, for it works in the power of the Spirit.

## Evidences of the Spirit at Work

*A vision of the growing opportunities* set before the teaching church is one evidence that the Spirit is at work. A human tendency is to center on what is at hand and to be content with a manageable objective. There is a fear of overextension and of tackling more than can be handled. "Count the cost" is the watchword of an inherent conservationism. By contrast, when the church is aware of the work of the Spirit in its midst, it is more bold and begins to dream. It sees the emerging challenges. It is sensitive to the persons who are in need of ministry. The church begins to consider how its ministry can be expanded. It recognizes that the Great Commission to teaching knows no limits. It is captivated with a vision of how it might enable men and women to grow as new persons in Christ. The church moves beyond its immediate situation to engage in an expanding ministry to reach more persons and to deepen the quality of the learning experiences that it offers. A vision of ministry is one of the clear evidences that the Spirit is at work in the church.

A second evidence of the Spirit's ministry is the *attitude of openness* to learning. Closed minds and unresponsive hearts block the work of the Spirit in the teaching ministry. Whenever the church has attempted to lock the truth into a rigid form, life and vitality have been lost. Such times have been among the darkest periods in the history of the church. God's truth is growing and expanding, with exciting new discoveries waiting to be made. Only minds that are alert to the possibilities of seeking that truth in new ways and in deeper dimensions give the Spirit the opportunity to work. The teaching church never believes that it has "arrived." Rather, it continues to struggle to discover all it can of God's will and purpose for its mission in the world. Openness and receptivity are signs that it remains sensitive to the leading and direction of the Spirit.

Yet another evidence of the work of the Spirit is the *commitment of the church to its teaching ministry.* Commitment is expressed in the time, energy, and resources devoted to this ministry. When the church is truly convicted of something, that conviction is normally reflected in its order of priorities. It means little to claim that the education program of a church is important unless the claim is borne out in the commitment that the church is ready to make to that program. The church with a vision of the significance of its teaching ministry will gladly and freely invest itself and its resources in making the ministry a priority. The Spirit cannot bless and prosper efforts made begrudgingly and reluctantly. Rather, the Spirit moves when the church freely and joyously gives itself and its possessions to the furtherance of God's work.

The best evidence of all that the Spirit is working is *the presence of changed lives*. The familiar image of birth in the story of Nicodemus serves to remind us of the amazing change in the life touched by the Spirit. Jesus spoke of this change as rebirth. Puzzled, Nicodemus pressed Jesus for an explanation of how one can be born a second time. Jesus told him that a second birth is produced by the Spirit. The story does not tell us the response of Nicodemus to this truth, but the account remains to teach us what happens when the Spirit makes persons alive to God.

The teaching ministry of the church is never limited to the transmission of content and the acquisition of knowledge, but, rather, is directed to the transformation of persons and their subsequent nurture. It seeks to call into being new creations in Christ Jesus. When persons are changed into new beings, this is not an accomplishment of the church nor of any individual. It is the work of the Holy Spirit and the gift of God. There is mystery here, because no one commands or controls. As Jesus said, "The wind blows where it wills, and you hear the sound of it, but you do not know whence it comes or whither it goes; so it is with every one who is born of the Spirit" (John 3:8).

## Gifts for Teaching

All persons possess gifts that are special to them. These gifts take many forms, and they serve to reflect the uniqueness of persons. The New Testament talks about them as "gifts of the Spirit." We do not produce them; they are given to us. If they are neglected or misused, they are lost. In the words of Paul in his letter to the Ephesians, their use is "to equip the saints for the work of ministry, for building up the body of Christ, until we all attain to the unity of the faith and of the knowledge of the Son of God, to mature manhood, to the measure of the stature of the fulness of Christ" (Ephesians 4:12-13).

There are special gifts given to the church for the ministry of teaching. No gift is greater perhaps than the ability to listen. The church can never teach effectively until it has first listened. If it does not first listen, it may simply answer questions that have never been asked. Effective ministry with persons begins with listening to them.

Listening enables one to become aware of persons as they are—with their doubts, their questions, their problems, and their needs. Instead of the church proceeding on untested assumptions, it will, by listening, get specific information from persons. They become real persons with their own particular needs. Listening to persons is the first step in knowing them. Until one-to-one relationships are established, persons are really being treated as objects or things. As always, our model is Jesus who listened to persons as he dealt with them. People have a great hunger and need to be listened to. Being truly heard is a means of being affirmed as human beings who matter. This human affirmation is a necessary step toward discovering that God loves and affirms persons.

The gift of listening is the means of discovering people's real needs. Persons do not always understand what their real need is, and the skilled listener may be able to cut through superficial issues and come to grips with the fundamental issue or need. When a rich young man asked Jesus one day about the secret of eternal life, he talked about what was expected of him. Obviously this was a choice young man with whom Jesus was deeply impressed. However, Jesus did not stop with what appeared on the surface; he cut to the core. The problem for this man was love of possessions. This was the block that the young man was not able to deal with, and the story tells us that he went away sorrowful. Skillful listening includes the ability to hear what may lie behind a person's words.

The church needs to utilize fully the gift of listening. Adults sometimes forget how important it is to listen to children. All children need to feel that adults listen to and hear them. One of the great gifts any teacher can bring to the classroom is the ability to hear each individual as a special and unique person. The church that places a high premium upon the gift of listening is wise.

An equally important gift of the Spirit is the gift of caring. The teaching church is most effective when it is most caring. The message of God's redeeming love has to be expressed in a ministry that demonstrates that same redeeming quality. Love is not a quality to be talked about in abstract terms but, rather, one to be lived out with power and grace. The teaching ministry is a ministry of love and caring, of actually loving rather than merely teaching about loving.

Caring expresses itself in many ways in the church. It begins by affirming that all persons are important. There can be no distinctions of age, gender, race, or station. The barriers between persons have been broken down and in Christ all people have been set free. The church teaches with great impact when it affirms and cares for each person within the fellowship. The church reveals what is possible by the power of the Holy Spirit when the love of Christ truly possesses every member. One of the things that impressed outsiders about the early believers was the love they had for one another. A sign that the Spirit is at work in the church is its quality of caring for its own.

The caring expresses itself beyond the immediate fellowship. The acid test for caring is the church's inclusiveness. Caring for one's own kind can be expected, but caring for those very different from oneself demands a special quality. The church's commission is not limited to a select group but includes all people everywhere. The church's task is worldwide and without boundaries. The Spirit grants this gift of caring for people simply because they are people. This powerful aspect of the church's teaching ministry obviously would never be possible apart from the special "infilling" from God. The church loves and cares because it knows itself first to have been loved.

The Holy Spirit also gives the church the gift of nurture. The teaching ministry is a ministry of nurture. Nurture is the long and patient process of helping the immature to grow to maturity. The spiritual pilgrimage of persons has many developmental stages, not unlike normal human development. There must always be the nourishment and support to maintain the growth process, lest the development be stymied or arrested. It is essential that the growing person have the support appropriate to the specific stage of development. Obviously, persons can be found at every possible growth point. Nurturing is possible because the more mature nurture the less mature, the strong care for the weak, and the experienced guide the less experienced. The image used in the New Testament is of a seed that is planted, watered, cultivated, and tended until it comes to full maturity. The Spirit is always at work in the nurturing process.

Nurture is a slow and time-consuming exercise. The results do not occur immediately; in fact, they frequently cannot be seen for years. The changes are not obvious except from the perspective of a long time frame. Patience is a special requirement of those who are nurturing. They require a strong measure of faith to believe that in due time the growth will be apparent. The teaching church has to gear itself up for the long haul and accept the fact that growing toward maturity takes time. Part of the Spirit's gift of the ability to nurture is the special quality of patient faithfulness.

## The Spirit As Teacher

It is quite impossible to conceive of the church's teaching ministry apart from the work of the Holy Spirit. The church can strive to open the door for the mystery of grace and faith. It can attempt to provide the atmosphere of openness and caring. It can share its own faith experience. The fact remains that it is only the Spirit who can bring into being the new person. The Spirit is the teacher and the church the co-teacher.

# 5

# The Teaching-Learning Community

Learning in the church takes place within the context of the community. Persons learn and grow when surrounded by a loving and caring community that nurtures and sustains them. The concept of community is foundational in the church's understanding of its teaching ministry.

It is helpful to remember that those first disciples Jesus drew around him had to share a common life for several years before they could begin to comprehend what his ministry was all about. The call that he gave them was a call into community. Day by day they learned to depend on God's grace. They became united in a fellowship unlike anything they had ever known. In time they found themselves together in God's mission in the world. What had been a group of diverse individuals was knit into a community with power and purpose. Jesus made the development of community a basic step in the creation of a teaching-learning experience. The teaching church affirms the necessity of building an effective teaching ministry on the foundation of community.

## Koinonia

When the New Testament speaks about the church, it is not referring to a building or structure but to a group of people. The church is people meeting for worship in someone's home. The church is a group of persons coming together to consider their faith. The word to describe such groups of people is the Greek word *koinonia,* which we translate "fellowship" or "community." This community has only one real distinction: its Lord. The presence of the living Christ at its center is what gives this community its uniqueness as well as its reason for being. Apart from this one distinction, it is like any other group of persons. Many groups claim to be fellowships or communities, but they are not *koinonia*.

The fellowship of the church is a unique creation. *Koinonia* is a community of men and women of many backgrounds and origins who are united by the fact that Jesus Christ is their Lord. The relationship with Christ makes possible this utterly new and transforming relationship with others who also follow Christ. *Koinonia* is built upon the relationship with Jesus Christ as Savior and Lord. There is no place for exclusiveness among those who have entered into this relationship. By their act of commitment to faith in Jesus Christ they are knit into the family of believers.

One of the distinctions of the community is its demands upon the total person. There is no provision for a partial commitment, a limited amount of time, or a portion of one's life. To accept Christ and enter into the community of faith is to accept a life calling. The commitment is to be a witness to him in every word, thought, and deed. What the world knows of Christ it will know through the witness of the community.

Not everything that is called fellowship in the church is, in fact, *koinonia*. Much of what is experienced in the church may not be genuine community at all. It may have the outward appearance but lack an inner quality that makes it a truly redemptive community. Many meaningful experiences having the sense of human togetherness do not reflect the true awareness of unity in Christ. Not every emotionally charged experience grows out of the transforming relationship to Christ. "Feeling good" is not a guarantee that one is experiencing *koinonia*. The sign of *koinonia* is the breakdown of disunity and the affirmation of unity in Christ. That which most profoundly impressed onlookers about the early church was the coming together of wealthy women, slaves, and soldiers in Christian love and oneness. Observers could find no rational explanation for such behavior; it ran counter to all the normal expectations of how persons of diverse backgrounds act toward one another. The onlookers did not know it, but they were witnessing the power of *koinonia*.

Our contemporary, predominantly urbanized life makes the achievement of community more difficult. Characteristically, the members of a church come from many communities, and when they assemble for worship on Sunday morning, they are almost like strangers to one another. In all likelihood they have not seen or talked with one another during the previous week. These realities make the task of discovering and building community extremely difficult.

The fact that *koinonia* may be difficult due to the wide dispersal of its people does not change the fact that the church functions as a community of believers. The concept of "people of God" is deeply rooted in Scripture. They are a people with a mission, as First Peter makes quite clear. The emphasis is on community, not on structure or institution. The community is special because the Spirit—who is essential for guidance, support, nurture, and faith renewal—dwells within it.

## Community Within Community

In close human interaction persons find community. Most significant human interaction takes place in smaller units where there can be face-to-face encounters. The church is made up of a series of smaller experiences of community where persons have opportunities to be with a limited number of other persons on a more intimate basis. These can take many forms: support groups, study groups, circles, house meetings, prayer fellowships, and church school classes. These small groups, whatever their form, become a focus for the life of the congregation.

Studies have shown that persons find it very difficult to relate to an entire congregation. Unless they can be identified with some small group in the church, the likelihood is great that they will not maintain an active relationship with the body. A small group provides a manageable number of interpersonal relationships. The individual becomes more important because others know his or her name. There is more special interest directed to the individual. The presence and participation of each individual becomes significant. In a small group each absence is noticed. The involvement in the smaller unit enables one to be an active participant in the larger community.

The teaching church depends upon its classes and groups to provide the formal occasions for teaching-learning. It seeks to group persons, or in many cases permits them to group themselves, according to age, interest, or felt need. The teaching church recognizes that persons reflect a great many differences. At the same time, it accepts the fact that commonality attracts persons to one another.

Classes and groups are natural expressions of human relationships. With time they develop an identity and a life of their own. Like people, they have a life span of birth, adolescence, maturity, decline, and death.

becomes warped and the original intent for which they were formed is forgotten. They have the unfortunate capacity to become ingrown. When this happens, the group is so rigidly defined that outsiders are excluded. The group is fixed and wants no changes. Least of all does it want its complacency disturbed. When a situation like this develops, it is a sign that the bond with the larger community has been eroded, if not erased.

Classes and groups are not formed for their own pleasure and comfort but to prepare the members for the tasks they face as Christians in the world. The purpose of small groups and the larger community is to equip members for mission in the world. The whole community struggles against focusing inwardly; it must keep its vision directed outward.

The community can grow effectively through the establishment of new groups. It is easier to get persons into new groups than to have them attempt to break into established ones. New groups have a much stronger will to grow, and therefore they tend to grow. (Studies have shown that once established groups reach an optimum size, their capacity to grow beyond that size is virtually nonexistent. The members of such a group often find this incapacity difficult to accept and on occasion will oppose the formation of new groups that are viewed as competitive.) More people will be reached and involved if new groups are established than if existing groups are compelled to add to their numbers.

While the teaching church elects to function through its smaller units, it has to retain the responsibility for maintaining the larger vision of its mission. The parts, or groups, must be melded together as a whole. No part can claim to stand alone and deny its interdependence. It must see its small ministry as integrally related to the whole teaching ministry. Classes or groups that become "little churches" in their own right are denials of the true meaning of the Christian community. The Body of Christ is one, and all its parts must reflect the oneness of the indwelling Spirit.

## The Redemptive Community

A very significant quality of the Christian community is its redemptive capacity. It impacts upon the lives of persons in ways that change them. It provides the nurturing context in which persons of all ages are enabled to grow and develop. Its rule is the rule of love. Love has the power to make life different.

The New Testament describes love as a quality of relationship that seeks to act toward others as Christ has acted toward us. Learning can undoubtedly take place in the absence of love, but experience shows again and again that persons learn best in an atmosphere of love and concern. Learning is helped by love and hindered by fear. As the writer in First John reminds us, "There is no fear in love, but perfect love casts out fear" (1 John 4:18). The freeing power of love makes persons open to learning. A person must first discover his or her value by being affirmed by another. The great discovery that God can and does love us begins with a loving person helping us to experience love and acceptance.

The redemptive community does not simply teach persons about the Christian experience in the way that other knowledge is taught, for the essence of the Christian experience can never be taught. Rather, it must be caught. It cannot be reduced to a list of rules or perceptions; it is more than a pattern of conduct. Christian experience passes mysteriously from one life to another when the Spirit of God moves upon the scene. A person must first become aware of his or her value as a person who is worthy of love, specifically God's love. Such awareness cannot be taught in the ordinary sense but, rather, God's love must be experienced. One learns to be Christian by being part of the Christian community. A book published some years ago entitled *You Can't Be Human Alone* echoes this fact. It is the community that is redemptive and transforming. The individual must be part of the community to make the discovery of what it means to be a new creation in Jesus Christ.

The redemptive community has a number of qualities which persons need to experience so as to grow in the Christian faith. Its greatest quality is *acceptance*. Acceptance implies taking people as they are, recognizing their worth, and communicating that recognition. It is a quality that is easier to talk about than to possess. It is one thing to say that we accept everyone and another thing to live a life of acceptance. It is always easier to respond to certain individuals than to others. As visitors come to the church our minds unconsciously classify those who belong and those who do not. We identify certain people as being like ourselves while others, well, they are simply different. Acceptance means being able to rise above any categories of human differences and to see persons as persons with God-given worth. The church does not always rise to this level; instead it draws the lines of exclusion. It establishes its own criteria for those it will accept into its company. Often these criteria, though implicit and unexpressed, operate nevertheless with great effectiveness. The church is truly the redemptive community when it draws no lines and when it warmly and happily accepts all who come. To do less is to condition love and to deny human worth. The unqualified acceptance of all persons is the hallmark of the redemptive community.

The redemptive community is likewise characterized by its spirit of *openness*. It is free of pretense and subterfuge. It never claims to be something it is not. To hold the Christian community up as a kind of model for the rest of society is not appropriate. It understands itself in terms of brokenness made whole. The reason that it can welcome persons of every condition or background is that it knows its own state to be one of brokenness and imperfection. The Christian community is not ideal in terms of perfection but in the Hebrew sense of wholeness, which accepts the discordant, alienated aspects of life within a community.

Openness is the ability of persons in the community to communicate on the deepest levels utterly without pretense. The truth spoken in love is normative. The deepest and most troubling issues of life can be discussed with total candor. No longer does conversation need to remain merely polite and superficial. When a person is hurting, the open and free recognition of and response to that hurting is anticipated. When persons are able to admit their own frailties and needs and share these with others, love and support can begin the healing process. The church is a redemptive community when it maintains this openness to its own true nature. It is at its best when it understands itself as a community of brokenness in the process of being made whole. At the heart of its life is forgiveness, understanding and grace. It guards against thinking of itself more highly than it ought to think. It remembers that its hope is in the healing ministry of the Spirit.

When the community is redemptive, it also has the quality of *trust*. Persons can grow when there are other significant persons in their lives in whom they can place their trust. Trust brings the freedom to explore life and to venture into the untried and the unknown.

Currently, some fascinating programs are set up to teach infants to swim. The results are quite amazing, and one has to be impressed to see very small children paddling around in the water with complete freedom and obvious enjoyment. They learn quickly and easily what adults find difficult. The secret is trust, which comes naturally to these infants. The presence and support of the parent or teacher helps the children to discover that the water is also supportive and dependable. Out of that relationship of trust is born the confidence to handle this new experience. The children can learn quickly because they have complete trust. There is no fear, no holding back, no lack of confidence.

Unfortunately the passage of the years erodes this ability to trust, an ability that frequently has to be relearned in maturity.

Trust is necessary for Christian growth to take place. There are risks in the pilgrimage of faith with which a person can never cope apart from an undergirding of trust. The absence of trust is debilitating and destructive. It produces fear, loss of confidence, and uncertainty. The lack of trust prevents a person from achieving what is actually within his or her capacity. Trust works in both directions. On one hand, trusting allows a support system of dependable and secure relationships to develop; on the other hand, being trusted gives a person a sense of worth and dignity. To trust and to be trusted are essential factors in the human growth process. The redemptive community establishes the context in which trust can be experienced and developed.

Another essential quality in growth which the community offers is *freedom*. There is room for persons to develop in their own unique ways. Individuality is affirmed. Not everyone has to look and act the same. Differences in persons are important and worthy of acknowledgment. Uniqueness can and ought to be celebrated.

Be forewarned about efforts to impose conformity in the church. It is easy to describe what one conceives as normative. Once such a standard is established, it is also relatively easy to ascertain whether persons do or do not conform to the standard. Those who don't are forced into a mold. Persons who do the forcing often find variety disturbing. They like to have others think, speak, and act exactly like themselves. Conformity becomes the ultimate objective. Some of the cruelest and most vindictive periods in the church's history have been times when a part of the organized church persecuted and destroyed persons whose chief crime was that they did not fit the accepted mold. Obviously there are less extreme expressions of the limits upon freedom to retain one's individuality; for example, some groups set up rigid criteria and admit to membership only those who will accept those criteria without reservation. Such groups take pride in their exclusiveness. This is not at all what it means to experience the true freedom of a redemptive community.

Inclusiveness is the true character of the redemptive community. Persons who are very different in many ways can be free to remain themselves while being bound together by their common allegiance to the living Lord. One of the great witnesses to the transforming power of the gospel is its ability to attract into one fellowship of faith the most amazing variety of persons with contrasting backgrounds. The glory of the freedom found in such fellowship is that no one has to be pressed into a mold to fulfill the expectations of others. It is unfortunate that many churches we know do not always exemplify that quality of freedom. They are basically made up of one kind of people. The excitement of knowing, working with, and caring for persons who are different from themselves is missed. Sadly, the church is not always as free as it might be.

This redemptive community, which is the body of Christ, is characterized by its acceptance, its openness, its trust, its freedom, and, above all, its love. Love is the dynamic that energizes all its activities. Love is the force that brings about the healing and the movement toward wholeness. Love brings into being a new community in which persons are valued for themselves. This quality of life brought about by love commends the church to the world, and when the church fails in this purpose, the world condemns it. It is to be remembered that the most important justification of the church's life is never the perfection of its members as much as its ability to point beyond itself to God.

## Informal and Unplanned Teaching

The community of faith has its formal, planned, intentional program of education. It is very easy to equate these structured efforts with the sum of what the church is teaching. The fact of the matter is that a very large part of what the church teaches is totally unplanned and unintentional. The church does some of its most powerful teaching when it is not even thinking about it. Teaching is more than words and lessons. It is reflected in the whole life of the community, in its attitudes, its values, its sense of mission, and its actions. In a sense, the church teaches far more by what it does than by what it says.

Picture for a moment a scene that can be duplicated in city after city across the country. The neighborhood is in transition. New residents are moving in to replace the families that have gone to the developing suburbs. The neighborhood had been predominantly white and now is ethnically diverse. First Church stands on the corner where it has stood for more than seventy-five years. The building reflects the day when it served a large and prosperous congregation. The congregation is now small, and its activities are very limited. The remaining members are faithful, and they come in on Sunday morning from other areas of the city. Although the bulletin board outside says "Welcome," no one from the neighborhood attends. When the service is over, the folk leave, the doors are locked for another week, and the building stands dark and empty. It is a dismal picture and one that is easier to put out of mind than to try to ask the hard question about what the picture means and what it is telling us.

It may be assumed that some faithful teaching takes place on those Sunday mornings for the faithful that gather. The experience may be very meaningful, and the persons may go away strengthened in their faith. They may find this little community of faith an important resource for living. They may have a very significant ministry of love and caring for one another. The church is obviously teaching the members of the congregation much more than can be communicated in lessons or sermons. Week by week persons are learning more about what it means to be part of the body of Christ by simply being a part of that body. But is this all that this church teaches? What is it teaching its neighborhood?

The answer is that it may be doing a great deal of negative teaching that it never intended to do. It may be saying, "This church belongs to us, as it belonged to our parents before us, and not to you." It may be saying, "We do not really have anything to offer to you." It may be saying, "We have never stopped to think of ways in which we might serve and minister to this neighborhood." It may be saying, "We are not concerned that the building stands dark and empty all week."

What might be some of the words that persons in the neighborhood would use to describe their feelings about old First Church? They could be words like snobby, uncaring, self-satisfied, unconcerned, and out-of-touch. Some harsher words could be racist or bigoted. Unintentionally this church may have communicated only negative images. It may have taught a whole neighborhood that there really is not any good news for the persons living there. It may have taught more powerfully than it can imagine without ever realizing what it was doing.

The teaching church must always remember that its witness to the world involves the unplanned as well as the planned. Its actions and its deeds as well as its words communicate the message. When those actions and deeds do not live up to the words, they in all probability still leave a lasting impression. The church is on display when it is at its worst as well as its best. It chooses the times when it does its formal, planned teaching, but it never knows when it is teaching in unplanned and informal ways.

Likewise, there is much teaching that goes on within the church that is unintentional or unconscious. Children in some churches learn early that the church is for adults. The adults end up in the most attractive rooms and have the most comfortable chairs. Worship services that are supposedly for the whole community of faith are almost entirely oriented to adults. Children learn in church school classes, but they also learn through the attitudes they encounter, the actions they experience, and the values they see honored.

Young people often struggle to find their place in the church. They are told they are wanted, but at the same time they are made to feel that they are welcome only as long as they conform to certain standards laid down by adults. Tensions can develop between young people and adults over the use of the church building. On occasion adults give the impression that respect for a building is a higher priority than respect for persons. They may not say this outright, but the young people go away with the feeling that they are simply tolerated by adults *claiming* to want them in the church, yet *demonstrating* it in a strange way. Words are not enough to make young people feel that the church is truly theirs. Indeed, unplanned, unintentional teaching can be powerful.

The facilities that a church provides (or fails to provide) can say much about its concern for persons with special needs. A ramp can say one thing to the person in a wheelchair, and the lack of a ramp can communicate something quite different. An amplifying system for the hearing impaired gives one message; the absence of a system gives a different message. In the minds of some church members these matters may seem inconsequential, but to the persons in need of such aids, nothing could be more important. In these very concerns about people, the church is teaching what it really believes about responding to the needs of people. Again, deeds have a far greater impact than words.

The community must come to terms with the reality of this informal, unplanned, unintentional learning. Its teaching is continuous in terms of word, thought, and deed. Unfortunately it does not teach simply when it is at its best but also when at its worst. Whenever the church attempts to hide behind its words and ignore the impact of its example, it is in deep trouble. Often its words are never heard—only its example is seen. The responsibility the community of faith is asked to assume is heavy; it must live out before the whole world that which it claims to believe. The quality of life of the community is in many ways the most powerful teacher of all.

"You are the light of the world. A city set on a hill cannot be hid. . . . Let your light so shine before men, that they may see your good works and give glory to your Father who is in heaven" (Matthew 5:14-16).

# 6

# The Teaching-Learning Process

The teaching church's educational process can be formal and structured or informal and unstructured. One way or the other, that process is foundational to the church's teaching ministry. It has to do with the way in which the church elects to address its educational tasks. If the church wants to be purposeful and intentional about its tasks, then establishing specific guidelines becomes imperative. Even when there is resistance to formalizing the process, a church operates with certain presuppositions and positions which become determinative. Every teaching program builds upon some kind of foundational process.

## Variety of Starting Points

There is a broad diversity of opinion among churches as to the starting point for the teaching-learning process. For some, the point of beginning has to be rooted in the authority of the Bible. The Sunday school movement in American Protestantism has traditionally believed this point. The development and use of a cooperative, uniform lesson series, which has functioned for over one hundred years, symbolizes that commitment to Scripture as the starting point. The Bible deals with humanity's spiritual needs and can be the only basic textbook for the study of faith and life. The aim of education is to provide knowledge and guidance so that sinful humanity will be led to repentance and conversion. The Bible, then, provides all that is needed for the nurture and development of persons as they move toward Christian maturity. The content of Christian teaching has to be in harmony at all points with the authority of the Bible. For those whose starting point is the

Scriptures, the answer to the question "What is the purpose of your educational program?" will be "To teach the Bible."

A contrasting position is represented by those who place the emphasis upon the authority of the church. For them the church is the starting point for the educational process because God has conferred upon the church alone the right to teaching along with an infallibility in matters of faith and morals. This does not discount the authority of Scripture. It simply places Scripture under the power of the church to interpret and direct. Writings, pronouncements, actions of the church over the centuries comprise the body of ecclesiastical authority. This great body of tradition belongs to the church, which in turn means that only the church can teach. The purpose of the educational program is the transmission of church tradition. Little room is left for deviation, and anything that falls outside that particular body of tradition is labeled error.

A third approach makes its starting point human experience. This position does not necessarily deny the importance of the Bible or tradition but, rather, states that the logical place in an educational process to begin is with the person. It recognizes the insights that have come through studies of the formation of personality and general human development. This position accepts the validity of human experience as a foundation for learning. It insists that an understanding of human nature can come from observation and the behavioral sciences. It senses a continuity of human knowledge and experience, of which religious knowledge and experience are a part. Christian educators have been deeply influenced by this perspective which arises out of the scientific method. The purpose of an educational program that initiates learning in the realm of experience is to put the person in the center and then to address the issues that grow out of this person's specific situation.

Conflicts arise out of the tensions among these three starting points. Charges are hurled back and forth. The fact is that each point has elements of truth and a contribution to make. The wise course is to appreciate each one and to avoid being locked into one uncompromising position. It is probably true that the church has always reflected a variety of approaches to its educational task.

## Lifelong Learning

A basic concept of education in the church is lifelong learning. The community draws no lines between the immature and the mature; everyone needs to learn and to keep on learning. Granted, there may be many levels of learning—but it *is* learning. The classic statement comes in the words of the Apostle when he says,

> "Not that I have already obtained this or am already perfect; but I press on to make it my own, because Christ Jesus has made me his own. Brethren, I do not consider that I have made it my own; but one thing I do, forgetting what lies behind and straining forward to what lies ahead, I press on toward the goal for the prize of the upward call of God in Christ Jesus" (Philippians 3:12-14).

The wisest of teachers are at the same time learners. It may be fair to say the best teachers always recognize that they never move beyond the role of learner. Their pupils sometimes become their teachers. This interplay of roles is a tremendously helpful picture of the ongoing nature of the learning experience. No one ever knows so much that there is no more to be learned. The community of faith is a community of learners. This important truth prevents the development of an elite group that elevates itself above the rank and file and takes pride in its superiority. The unfinished nature of the learning task is a stimulant to continued growth and an antidote to stagnation.

The concept of lifelong learning helps to structure the organization of the church. The educational program is not an optional function of the church but a basic reflection of what the church is called to be. To speak of the teaching church is not to refer to one of its primary activities but rather to describe it as a community of persons who are called by God to continue throughout their lives to grow.

## Developing Persons

Lifelong learning implies that the educational process covers the entire life span from cradle to grave. To be effective, the process has to take into account the stages of human development. It has to recognize the significant differences between the immature and the mature. It simply has to understand how persons grow.

The religious experience of the child is different from that of the adult, but each experience has its own integrity and validity. There was a time when children were regarded as merely little adults. They were expected to have the same experiences and the same understandings as adults. We recognize now that not only is this untrue, but it also violates the nature of the child. There is a delightful eagerness with children to experience new things, but those new ideas or activities can be incorporated only at the level of their experience and understanding. The child always starts from the point where he or she is and moves from there. There are tremendous differences in children themselves. Not all ten-year-olds are alike. The church in its educational program must recognize that persons are unique and must be taught accordingly. One of the purposes for grouping children by ages and backgrounds into small groups is to try to teach them at their level of readiness.

Children are most comfortable with concrete thinking. When adults use abstractions, children become confused. If adults insist, children will use the abstractions, but they won't understand the meanings. In working with children, adults must be careful to remember that children are very literal. Words bring to mind concrete images. Abstract thinking is a stage of development that they have not yet reached. Because of the many abstract concepts in the Christian faith, the church has a special responsibility to protect children from attempts to teach them what they may not yet be ready to learn.

Wide disagreement exists concerning what children are ready to learn. A number of very competent Christian educators contend that the church often starts doctrinal instruction too early. They remind us that the fact that children learn to use certain words or to repeat specific doctrinal phrases does not mean that they comprehend this information. These scholars fear that persons grow into maturity without ever developing a mature understanding of the concepts they theoretically learned as children. We are reminded in the words of Paul, "When I was a child, I spoke like a child, I thought like a child, I reasoned like a child . . ." (1 Corinthians 13:11). The arguments will undoubtedly continue, but the fact remains that the church should never expect children to have adult experiences.

Childlike faith is beautiful, and children have the marvelous capacity for wonder and awe. Their openness and trust are qualities to be cherished. One hopes that some of those capacities can be preserved in the growth process. Our perception of truth must mature and develop while, ideally, we remain childlike and open.

At a certain point the child moves into adolescence and becomes part of the wonderful world of youth. Youth is a period of searching and testing—a person is neither child nor adult, but at times a bit of both. Characteristically, adolescence is the time when commitment is made to Christ and the church. In this period faith moves from the level of the child to a new depth of understanding where it can be appropriated as one's own.

One characteristic of youth is intense loyalty to friends and perhaps to family. As youth mature, that circle of loyalties expands. Youth begin to discover themselves in relation to a world larger than they have previously known. It is at this point that the church has a great opportunity to help shape their loyalties and to establish their ultimate loyalty to God. It is very critical that those adults who work with the youth and who often become focal points for their loyalty be mature role models that youth can respect and from whom they can learn. It is not always an easy time in the life of the church when the intensity of the young people's loyalties and commitment comes into tension with the tepid attitudes and staid behavior of many adults. Growth can be painful and difficult, not only for the person growing but for those around as well. Testing limits and confronting accepted practices are ways that young people search out the nature of truth for themselves. Adults should understand and accept this, but unfortunately this is not always the case.

Persons have to do their own learning. To do this, they require freedom, which includes the freedom to fail. There has to be a certain amount of trial and error. Adults do not always find it easy to permit this kind of trial and error to happen, and their intrusion frequently results in conflict. It is not easy for adults to refrain from trying to control youth when the former are certain that they know better. The church has to learn to live with this tension between youth and adults—for the sake of peace and tranquility—because the failure to do so could stifle the growth process. The church has to insure the human freedom to try and to fail as a very necessary component of the process of persons learning for themselves. As new beliefs, convictions, or understandings evolve, young persons have to try them out before they can make them their own.

In the same wonderful and mysterious way that persons move from childhood into adolescence, they move from adolescence into adulthood. Adults, like children and young people, are also at many different developmental stages. In our keeping with the concept of lifelong learning, they are to be considered learners. They are not closed to new experiences but tend to be more discriminating about new encounters than youth simply because they have a much broader frame of reference.

Generally, adults are at the stage of developing a pattern or system of values appropriate to their individual situations. Adults are expected to have developed some life goals that are instrumental in giving specific direction to their lives. They are also expected to be putting together their perspectives about life and their own value system. With adulthood comes the full awareness of personal identity and one's own role in relation to God, nature, and society. A fully mature religious experience is not possible until the sense of personal identity is completely developed. The educational process moves from the point at which faith is borrowed to the point at which it is fully owned. Not every adult reaches that point. Research is being done on the subject of adult faith development. Different researchers have their ways of describing the stages of faith development, but all agree that there is a broad spectrum of development, ranging from the very immature and simplistic to the highly sophisticated and mature. Age and experience have an influence upon the stages of faith development, but they are by no means determinative. One does not necessarily become mature in the Christian faith because one has lived a long time. Age is no guarantee of spiritual growth.

The church's educational task with adults is to foster a continuing developmental process, to assure that adults do not suffer from arrested development. Adults do not always feel the need for growth, and some of them easily become the victims of complacency. They require stimulation and motivation to prevent them from stagnating. The battle against inertia is ongoing. If adults are to retain an active participation in the church's educational program, their interest and imagination have to be stimulated. There has to be a very clear recognition that adults reflect a wide variety of backgrounds and experiences. The church's educational program must demonstrate sensitivity to a range of needs and diversity of backgrounds and experiences. All adults are learners, but their readiness to learn and their needs to learn have to be addressed with deep awareness of the diversity of approaches that are represented. The one thing that must be avoided at all costs is lumping all adults into one mass and ignoring their individual differences in the course of program development.

The church is made up of a great variety of persons of all ages and stages of development. All are equally important, and all have their place. The task of the teaching ministry is to see them as individuals and to plan for them accordingly. The goal is to enable each one to attain the highest degree of spiritual maturity possible. Children, youth, and adults—all developing persons—come together to form the community of learners.

## Methods for Effective Learning

There are ways of working with persons that enhance the effectiveness of the learning experience. Good teaching methods are important because they make it easier for persons to learn. When methods are properly selected, they become helpful tools for accomplishing educational goals. They are just tools, however, and work only when used by a skilled teacher.

The first characteristic of good teaching methods is that they *involve the learner.* Persons learn best when they participate most fully in the learning experience. Passivity is the one thing to be avoided at all costs, and the teacher who is content with a passive class makes a most serious mistake. Persons live in an atmosphere of give-and-take. Each person needs to bring something to the teaching-learning situation. The more one is involved in the experience, the more open one is to new insights and learnings. Good teaching-learning is always a two-way encounter between teacher and learner. There are many ways to offer active participation to learners: listening, answering questions, discussing, planning, observing, writing, taking a field trip, and doing a project. Careful planning is required so that no activity becomes an end in itself. Remember, the purpose of an activity is to help fulfill a specific learning objective, and such fulfillment becomes more effective when persons can be active participants in the learning experience.

A second characteristic of good teaching methods is that they *provide variety.* Constant repetition can destroy the effectiveness of even the best method. Learning is stimulated when fresh approaches catch the imagination and intrigue the interest. Variety is important not only because it helps in maintaining interest, but also because some methods are better suited than others for certain kinds of learning. A well-organized lecture on breadmaking may provide helpful information, but persons who want to learn how to make bread need the hands-on experience of making and kneading the dough. The same holds true in learning about the Christian faith: lectures are not enough. A variety of methods are required to give the learner a sense of creative participation and involvement in what he or she is learning.

In speaking about the ways of enhancing more effective learning, teachers always need to remember that the responsibility ultimately lies with the learner. Teachers can never learn for other people. People must learn for themselves. Teachers can offer the most exciting opportunities and can set up optimal conditions, but they are powerless to go beyond those measures. Learners take or leave what they are offered. They appropriate the teaching for themselves or they reject it. The outcome of any teaching-learning situation is unpredictable. Even the most carefully designed methods are no guarantee of success. To complicate the issue a bit more, unplanned learning can occur that the teacher had never intended. Confronted with new experiences, persons can respond in any number of ways. Learning is individual and personal and reflects the uniqueness of persons.

It is essential that the church's teaching approaches be consistent and integrated. Central to the development of the growing person is the need for harmony, stability, and inner unity. All experiences offered in the learning process have to be taken by persons and somehow made their own. When an individual appropriates a new learning for himself or herself, it has to become a part of the body of faith experience that the person already has. It means adjusting, changing, and struggling to find that inner harmony and stability. This process can be overwhelming and bewildering, especially when new learnings do not appear to relate to prior experience or understandings. Continuity and consistency of teaching throughout the church's educational program help to keep the learning process as positive and supportive as possible.

## Planning for Results

An effective educational program requires a clear sense of direction and a specific purpose. There are many directions and purposes from which to choose. No one church can do everything; so it must decide what it will do. Only when the church is prepared to state clearly and precisely what it intends to do has it established a basis for evaluating its teaching effectiveness or ineffectiveness.

Chapter 1 presented a discussion of the broad, overall goal for the church's educational ministry. Such a goal statement attempts to describe the end result, the hoped-for outcome of the total program. Growing out of that general goal are objectives that describe the more immediate and measurable results to be achieved. Foundational to any plan for a teaching ministry is the development of a set of objectives that sets forth what is to be accomplished.

Statements of objectives need to be clear and understandable. Their intentions need to be stated in very precise and exact terms. If they are to be the church's objectives, then it is essential that the whole church understand and accept them. If they require an explanation, they probably require rewriting.

Objectives need to be measurable so that it is possible to evaluate the degree of accomplishment. If the description of objectives is vague and indefinite, there is no way to know if what was desired did, in fact, happen. Numbers and dates give a specificity that makes it possible to measure results. Obviously, measurable objectives also must be realistic and attainable. They must be manageable in terms of what can be accomplished in the allotted time.

Good objectives for the teaching ministry will, of necessity, be person oriented. They will be concerned with what happens to the person. They will respect the developmental process and recognize the various stages of growth. They will recognize the importance of individual differences and the need for starting with persons where they are. They will be consistent with the best understanding of how persons learn and grow. Since the church's teaching ministry encompasses the life span from birth to death, its objectives will be comprehensive enough to cover the needs of all ages. The objectives will focus on the behavioral, the changes that take place in the persons' lives. They will be concerned with the attitudes and actions that evidence growth. Knowledge will not be transmitted for knowledge's sake, but for enabling persons to think and act in new ways. Developing behavioral objectives that will give proof of development toward Christian maturity is extremely difficult. Why? Because the task of determining religious or spiritual growth is a hard one. While measuring physical or intellectual growth is relatively easy, attempting to measure spiritual growth is the reason that the program of Christian education exists.

The process of the teaching ministry is most effective when it grows out of a clear plan that includes very specific objectives. A ministry with no objectives will wander in all directions. Knowing whether a program's destination has been reached will never be apparent because no one ever determined the destination. There is no shortcut for the provision of careful planning as a basic key to a successful educational program.

## Leadership—The Key Factor

The best designed and implemented educational plan, in the final analysis, depends upon the quality of its leadership. Only people can make a plan work. The more capable, the more committed, the more caring they are, the greater will be the effectiveness of the program. So much of the sharing of and learning about the Christian faith comes out of person-to-person relationship that there is no substitute for using the most experienced and mature persons within the community in the ministry of teaching. Those mature in the faith are best prepared to teach the less mature.

Congregations tend to end up with the kind of educational program that they deserve. If teaching is a low priority, the strongest leadership in the church will be diverted to other things. If it is a high priority and the church has a compelling awareness of its nature as a teaching-learning community, then leaders will give time and energy to this ministry.

It is a high calling for any follower of Jesus Christ to become a teacher within the community of faith. The teaching ministry is totally dependent upon the response of the faithful and committed women and men who acknowledge the implication of their call. It is a wise church who challenges, enlists, trains, commissions, and supports such persons. No truly effective educational program is possible without them.

# 7

# Worship and Celebration

At the heart of the life of the community of faith is the experience of corporate worship. In worship the church regularly affirms what it believes and celebrates the living presence of the Eternal One in its midst. For the members of a congregation, worship provides an unparalleled opportunity for learning.

Worship remembers and reenacts the gospel. The Good News is heard in terms of today's world and today's issues. God is at work in this world and its issues and makes known the redemptive power of divine love. Worship is God confronting us with the eternal message of grace and mercy as well as our response to that message. The reading and preaching of the written Word of God, the prayers and hymns, and the Lord's Supper become the occasion for God's living Word to be made known to us. God acted first and our response must follow. To conceive of worship as something done only to honor God is to miss the point entirely. To the contrary, worship is always a matter of opening up to what God has done and is doing in the midst of the church. The teaching church builds upon the opportunity to have persons experience learning on the most profound basis possible. Worship is one of the great elemental factors of the church's teaching ministry. Apart from any formal program of teaching, persons learn about the essence of the Christian faith by participating with other believers in worship. In places where religious activities are strictly controlled and formal educational programs forbidden, persons learn the deeper meanings of the faith by worshiping with other Christians. We normally do not equate worship with education, but it is educational at a very fundamental level.

## The Christian Year

A starting point for considering worship as a teaching-learning opportunity is the Christian year. The observance of high points in the church's calendar affords a structure for experiencing the story of redemption. The Christian year becomes, in this fashion, a very helpful teaching tool.

Advent season, commemorating Christ's birth, launches the year. Advent emphasizes the doctrine of incarnation, the astounding claim that God has come into the world in the form of a babe. None of the practices and activities that have grown up around Christmas overshadow the church's bold assertion that God has come in the flesh. The church needs to be careful that it does not become so enamored with the festivities of the season that it loses sight of the primary message it is to declare. Lovely customs of the holiday, as attractive and enjoyable as they may be, cannot be the church's focus. Rather, the celebration of God's great gift that comes to a sleeping, unaware world is the church's way of affirming the plan of redemption.

Epiphany, which is observed on January 6, signifies the visit of the wise men. The word "epiphany" literally means "manifestation." The coming of the wise men to Bethlehem symbolizes the sharing of the Good News of Christ's coming to the world. The wise men represent the world beyond the Jews for whom Christ is also Savior and Lord. Epiphany is a particularly appropriate time to emphasize the church's mission to the world.

The Lenten season has been observed in a variety of ways. In early Christian times Lent was associated with the practice of fasting prior to Easter. It was also a time of preparation for persons who were to be baptized on Easter. The emphasis has traditionally been on steps of preparation for the Easter event. Even when certain churches have done little by way of an official observance of Lent, there can be and often is a special emphasis on spiritual discipline. It is frequently a time for instruction or training classes.

While not a part of the Christian year historically, Race Relations Sunday in February is recognized by many churches as a significant teaching opportunity. The concern for human relationships across ethnic and racial lines is highlighted from the perspective of the gospel message.

Holy Week begins with the remembrance of Jesus' entry into Jerusalem on Palm Sunday and closes with the stark events of the crucifixion, death, and burial of the Lord. It is an intense period of preparation for the joyous celebration of Easter. In the observance of Good Friday, the focus is upon the awe and wonder of the suffering love exemplified in Jesus' death upon the cross. An opportunity to recall again the great events in the life of Jesus and the meaning of his coming to identify with humankind, Good Friday is one of the great teaching moments in the life of the church. A person cannot simply read about this event and understand the importance Christ's crucifixion has for the Christian community. One has to experience with the community of faith the anxiety and uncertainty of the first disciples as they faced those dark hours between the cross and the empty tomb. The ways in which the church observes and relives the events of the Passion Week become a kind of reenactment in which the disciples of today can and do take part. Holy Week is a very powerful and effective teaching-learning experience.

When the church celebrates Easter, it is affirming the very heart of its message to the world: Jesus Christ is the Lord of life. It is never possible to recapture fully what joy that first Easter must have brought to the disciples who had been plunged into gloom and despair by the tragic events of Good Friday. Yet there is no time when the church is able to sense and to communicate the joy of victory more than upon Easter morning. Many trappings have grown up around the Easter observance that have utterly nothing to do with the day. As with Christmas it is sometimes difficult to sort out that which is related to faith and that which may be part of an annual rite of spring. Despite this confusion, Easter is a great day for the church to proclaim its faith in the resurrected Lord. It is the day for the note of triumph to be sounded throughout the world.

Fifty days after Easter comes Pentecost, marking the coming of the Holy Spirit and the birth of the church. It originally marked the end of the fifty-day period following the Jewish Passover and was associated with the annual celebration of the grain harvest. Christians adopted Pentecost for the purpose of remembering the gift of the Holy Spirit and celebrating the life of the church. It has become a time to highlight the church's teaching on the doctrine of the Holy Spirit.

These observances, beginning with Advent and running through Pentecost, by no means exhaust the possibilities of the Christian year, but they do serve as superb teaching-learning opportunities for the teaching ministry of the church. They tie together the record of historical events with great doctrinal affirmations. In dramatic form they bring to life truths that can actually be experienced and consequently appropriated by those participating in the observances. The use of pageantry and the arts can communicate history and the faith in ways that go beyond the power of the spoken word. Impressions are made that remain with persons for a long time. A tremendously powerful impact is often made upon children who are caught up in the drama and the pageantry of different seasons. These times represent marvelous opportunities for the young persons to experience being part of the community as it affirms the very essence of its faith. The major festivals of the Christian year are teaching moments *par excellence*.

## Using Scripture in Worship

The systematic reading of Scripture in public worship is a method of teaching. The most common procedure is to use a lectionary that provides a three-year cycle of readings carefully selected from the Old Testament, the Epistles, and the Gospels. The selected readings relate to the season of the church year. Over the course of time they serve to focus the concerns of a congregation on the broad message of the Bible as revealed in its many parts. Systematic reading serves to guarantee that important passages of the Scriptures are not neglected while others are overused. The reading of the Scriptures becomes an intentional, well-designed program for familiarizing the hearers with the Word of God.

Obviously, the greatest value can come from the readings when there is a relationship between the Scripture and the sermon for the day. Passages can be chosen to highlight main themes in the Bible and Christian life, thus affording natural teaching opportunities if one elects to build upon them. It is never wise to assume that persons could not profit from some assistance in reflecting upon the meaning of the reading and its application to them. Beyond the immediate and literal interpretation is the theological perspective that has grown out of the church's experience. There is the understanding of how the passage relates to and addresses the fundamental issues and needs of human existence. The act of hearing Scripture in a service of public worship is in and of itself tremendously significant, but the experience is immeasurably enriched if it includes the opportunity for interpretation and amplification.

The reading of Scripture in public is an art. Not all worship leaders do it well. Careful advance preparation is a must. To hold the interest and attention of a congregation, a person must read with expression and vitality. The voice must be pleasant to listen to and easy to follow. The reading must be intelligent so that meaning is communicated to all. Stories must come alive to listeners. Poetry must be read as poetry so that the imagery can come through. The demeanor and deportment of the reader must unconsciously communicate the significance of the experience. Reading Scripture in a perfunctory fashion is unforgivable.

The effectiveness of Scripture in worship can be enhanced through variety. Even such a simple step as changing readers can be important. Well-trained lay leaders can make a significant contribution and can also witness to the fact that the Bible is the book of the whole church. Choric or antiphonal use of Scripture can powerfully and dramatically bring the message to the worshipers. Stories of the Bible lend themselves to dramatic treatment, which can have an impact on the eye as well as the ear. These stories can be of value in occasional unison reading by the congregation, particularly if time is taken for preparation.

I was impressed some years ago with the role of Scripture in the worship services of some churches in Eastern Europe. It was impressive to see how important the times of Bible reading were. Despite the barriers of language I was overwhelmed with the feeling of the significance of the experience. The practice was for the congregation to stand for the reading of the Word. The intensity of expression and the attentiveness of the listeners were extraordinary, the like of which is seldom experienced in many churches of the West. Perhaps the scarcity of Bibles among the congregation gave greater importance to the public reading. Perhaps the restrictions placed on their religious activities made the people more eager to take the fullest advantage of what was offered to them. Perhaps the cost of discipleship in this situation was high, and many of the worshipers had paid a price for their faith. Whatever the reason, the words "Let us hear the Word of the Lord" had a profound meaning to them, and they listened as if they were truly receiving a message from on high. I was left with the uncomfortable feeling that we in the churches in the so-called free world have missed something very important.

## Teaching Through Music

The faith of the Christian community is expressed in many forms of music. Music has been a chief means of expressing praise to God. It has the power to communicate the deepest feelings of the human spirit. It bridges the differences that separate people and provides a common experience of sharing. It is a tremendously effective teaching tool because of its ability to trigger the imagination and impress the memory.

The hymns of the church form the heart of the body of church music. They represent the centuries of efforts to express the central truths of the Christian faith. Their variety is diverse almost beyond imagination. The best of them bring together a strong text and an effective tune. Such hymns endure and can be sung meaningfully, generation after generation. Good hymns bridge the divisions of the church and are available to serve and bless persons everywhere.

When a congregation sings the hymns of faith, it is bearing witness to what it professes to believe. The music gives form and beauty to the profession in a way that deepens the participants' experience of faith. Music has the power to make them part of something larger than themselves and bestows the feeling of community. Congregational hymn singing is the finest possible opportunity to involve everyone. It helps persons to participate freely and move beyond a "spectator" religion. Such singing frequently makes a lasting impression, and the words and music of hymns sung many years before can be recalled with relative ease. The hymns that people know and love give a picture of the faith that they cherish.

In assisting persons to continue growing in faith, the hymns to which they are exposed must support and encourage that growth. The fact that people like a certain hymn is no guarantee that it has anything to contribute to growth. Congregations are frequently resistant to change and balk at the introduction of new or unfamiliar hymns. The process of introducing new hymns is an educational task. Steps need to be taken to assist a congregation in accepting them, e.g., providing clear and biblically based reasons for the choice of hymns. Congregations have to discover that God can still inspire hymn writers today. Newness does not remain a problem once people are convinced that a new hymn contributes to the understanding and expression of their faith.

Much about music is a matter of personal preference and taste. Some basic criteria, however, can be applied to all hymn texts and tunes. The text should be representative of and consistent with the best theological thinking and Christian teaching of the church. The images that the text conveys of God, Christ, the church, and the Christian life should be biblically based and sound in doctrine. The text should avoid the sentimental and introspective and should be a fit expression of praise to God. A hymn tune should reinforce the words of the text as well as be consistent with the nature of the text so as to give the feeling of a unified message. Music that has associations with nonchurch settings should not be used so that the music does not suggest any confusing connotations. Strong tunes reinforce the power of a hymn and let the congregation give glory to the Creator. Through its hymns the community of faith declares its faith and in the process appropriates the meanings of the hymns in a most significant learning experience.

The music offered by the choir on behalf of the congregation should likewise be consistent biblically and theologically with the doctrines of the church. The choir is an instrument for the praise and glory of God. Its calling is never to entertain the congregation or to render a performance for the sake of performing. The manner in which the choir sings and the impression made by its members communicate a clear message to those watching and listening. The great choral and instrumental music of the church can touch persons immensely. Hearing the classics of church music stretches the mind, warms the heart, and renews the spirit. Over a period of time the continuing experience of great church music enhances spiritual development and enriches the life of faith.

## Prayer in Worship

The community at prayer experiences the living presence of God and in so doing finds spiritual growth. Prayer that gives thanks for special joys in people's lives as well as petitions for those who are sick or troubled forms a bridge between worship and the concerns of everyday human existence. Persons discover ways in which their faith relates to life issues; a discovery which can be and often is an important learning process. Persons learn to pray by praying. Opportunities for them to participate in prayer in corporate worship teach them the practice of prayer. Conversely, the discipline of private prayer has a very significant relationship to what a person may discover in the experiences of prayer in worship. One of the great values of praying corporately is the broadening of the concerns for others that guards against prayer that is exclusively self-centered or self-serving. As one shares the richness of prayers for the community, a person enriches his or her own prayer experience. It is another example of how the community teaches through the quality of its corporate life.

One caution needs to be expressed about a possible misuse of prayer in congregational worship. Sometimes prayer is used to exhort the congregation. This use is prohibited. Prayer is not a device for telling persons what the leader may feel they need to hear; nor is it to be a little sermon directed at the congregation cloaked in the garb of prayer. Above all, it is not reproving people by addressing God. Any learning coming from such misuse is negative and counterproductive.

## Teaching Through Preaching

The preached word is an exposition of the written Word designed to reveal afresh the God who is revealed in Jesus Christ. God comes through the spoken word to the community of faith as the living and eternally present One. The purpose of the sermon is to make real in the contemporary setting the God who is revealed in the Bible. True preaching always seeks to establish the relationship of the written Word to the situation in which the congregation lives and moves. Not everything that comes from pulpits on Sunday mornings fits this description of preaching. Without an encounter with the living Word as revealed in the written Word, preaching in the classic Christian tradition has not taken place.

Preaching is an occasion for the community to discover God's will for its life. As the members of the congregation listen faithfully to the Word of God, they are reconciled to God and to one another. The preaching ministry gives them a growing sense of being incorporated into the body of Christ and of being equipped to bear witness for God in the world. Effective preaching educates the congregation over a period of time, because it systematically deals with the basic themes, central ideas, and principal teaching of the Scriptures. Effective preaching makes the congregation more biblically literate because it is consistently relating the written Word to the everyday life of the people. There is an element of mystery in preaching, for even though the sermon in and of itself may be faltering and seem inadequate at times, the listeners may still hear God's word. Paul called it "the foolishness of preaching." Preaching is obviously more than a human achievement in which something happens and persons know that somehow they have heard the voice of the Lord. In the ministry of the teaching church the preaching of the Word takes a place of central importance.

## Teaching Through the Sacraments

The sacraments, as enactments in the life of the church of God's redemptive acts, are occasions for learning. Through the use of common elements such as water, wine, and bread, the church sees how God has acted and is acting to bring about reconciliation.

The Word is made visible in the Lord's Supper which is observed in conjunction with the reading and preaching of the Word. In the service of Communion the congregation, through the use of bread and wine, remembers and gives thanks for the life, death, and resurrection of Jesus Christ. Communion is a celebration of the presence of the living Lord who now goes with them into the world. As the congregation goes, its members carry within their bodies the signs of his body and his blood. Thus, the service of Communion stands as the completion of the service of public worship. It is an act that symbolizes the unity of the Christian community and has the power to transcend barriers between persons. Even where differences of language and culture block communication, Christians of very different backgrounds can experience oneness in Christ as they break bread and drink the cup. The elements of the Communion bring the message of redemptive love to all who partake, irrespective of other communication barriers. The Lord's Supper is the enacted Word, in contrast to the written Word or spoken Word. The drama of God's grace and love is lived out in the worship experience of the community each time the bread is broken and the cup is shared, resulting in a powerful learning experience.

The ordinance of baptism throughout history has signaled entry into the faith community. It is the sign that one is a member of the body of Christ. It is said that in the early days of the church those in preparation for membership worshiped in the narthex of the building until after baptism. The baptistry itself was outside the church building. Only when persons had passed through the water of baptism were they allowed to enter the sanctuary and partake of the Lord's Supper. In this very meaningful symbolism the church witnessed the nature of membership in the body of Christ. The service of baptism is an enactment of death and resurrection and entrance into the church. It is a happy occasion that the church celebrates with joy. It presents a very meaningful opportunity for learning about the nature of commitment to Jesus Christ. Baptism's dramatic symbolism powerfully impresses all who participate with an open and receptive spirit.

## Guidelines for Worship

First, worship must be faithful in proclaiming the gospel so that persons will be confronted afresh with the living God. The story of God's mighty acts gives structure and content to Christian worship. Through the experience of worship the memory of those mighty acts is renewed. The criterion for judging worship is, therefore, its faithfulness to the story. Whatever does not recount and reflect the story does not belong in worship and should be eliminated. This standard of judgment needs to be applied to all aspects of worship. Do the hymns retell the story clearly and accurately? Does the choir music make an affirmation of faith? Is the sermon focused on the story or some part of it? Are the prayers responses of the congregation—in terms of praise, confession, thanksgiving, petition, and intercession—to the grace of God? Questions like these are needed as the congregation prepares to worship and seeks to be faithful to the story of Good News.

Second, worship must reflect the tradition from which it springs. It is not a matter of being slave to the past but of celebrating and lifting up the rich contribution of the predecessors of the faith. Part of a congregation's identity is connected to its corporate memory. In the church at large there is a very broad range of traditions reflecting the various paths that groups of Christians have followed. Corporate worship is the place where this rich diversity is most apparent. The diversity is an occasion for celebration, for it expresses the freedom found in Christ. Together the variety of worship patterns form a beautiful mosaic. Each pattern has its unique contribution to make. Conformity is not the ideal. Rather than seeking simply to be like everyone else, a congregation ought to rejoice in its own specific tradition and allow its worship patterns to affirm that tradition.

Third, worship must be set in the context of life today. Because it affirms and celebrates a tradition does not mean that worship can be clothed exclusively in the forms of the past. Worship must be in touch with today, though this does not mean that it reflects every fad of the moment. It does mean that it is connected to the significant events, the larger human issues, and life's persistent questions. People bring their world with them to worship, and the world that they bring cannot be ignored. Worship has to bring the sense of the divine into the mundane of everyday living. Worship that does not relate faith to life today is irrelevant.

Fourth, worship must relate to the whole person. The call of God is to the total being. We are to love God with heart and soul and mind. Worship deals with us as thinking, feeling, sensing beings. The difficulty for some persons is to involve their bodies. Inhibitions block the freedom to express themselves with their whole persons. We owe a profound debt of gratitude to the black tradition of worship, which demonstrates how we can participate as whole persons. The Creator who made us heart and soul, mind and body, deserves nothing less than the fullness of our beings in worship.

Fifth, worship must belong to everyone. It is an act of the congregation rather than of any leader. The members of the congregation are active participants, not spectators. Planning worship as well as participation in worship should have a congregational basis. The diversity of a congregation in age, experience, race, culture, and gender all must be taken into account. Worship that seeks to include all persons will be more open to the fullness and affirmation of God's glory than worship that excludes some persons.

The teaching church in its corporate worship discovers unparalleled opportunities to be a teaching and learning community. Worship provides some of the church's very best teaching.

# 8

# Faith Heritage

Our ancestry in the faith is an important dimension of the foundation of our teaching ministry. All of us build upon the heritage from which we have come. We reflect the beliefs and practices of our forebears. We are shaped by the traditions that we have inherited. A portion of the church's teaching task is to transmit its heritage to each succeeding generation.

An appreciation of heritage is important because it brings perspective to our faith. We understand the present better when we understand the past. Knowing from where we have come enables us to know where we are and where we are going. Just as roots are necessary to the flower, so roots are necessary for a living and growing faith. Without roots, faith does not survive.

## Many Roots, Many Branches

In an earlier chapter the unity of the church was discussed. There is one body, but there are many parts. From the beginning, Christians have lived and expressed their faith in diverse ways while seeking to maintain their unity in Christ.

The New Testament church experienced its diversity in many ways. Believers had different gifts: prophecy, service, teaching, giving, preaching. There were differing functions and roles: apostles, prophets, evangelists, pastors, teachers. Paul had to address the problem of competing loyalties between Apollos, Cephas, and himself. Through the centuries the church has had to continue to struggle with the issue of diversity and unity. The key to resolution has always been in terms of the symbolism of the church as a body, which remains one, though it has many members.

The proliferation of denominations since the first century gives the overwhelming feeling of diversity. The branches into which the church has divided are almost beyond counting. Attempts to merge or consolidate constantly struggle against the natural tendency to divide still further. The factors that give rise to these divisions are complex and confusing. The reasons may not be apparent or understandable to onlookers. From this process of branching emerges an ever-growing number of particular heritages, a contrast to the primary or basic heritage shared by the whole community of faith.

Great diversity frequently exists within a single denominational family. Various factors can make such a family reflect a whole spectrum of differences. Some factors will be related to regional backgrounds or ethnic and cultural origins. Others tie in with where people live: the inner city, urban and suburban neighborhoods, farms, or small towns. There are traditions within traditions. The pathways by which persons come to the Christian faith are many. The nature of Christian discipleship is influenced by this great variety of approaches and emphases. Two congregations bearing the same family label can easily have differences to the point that one may wonder how such diversity is possible among the members of a family. Again, there is the common heritage that stands in tension with that which is unique or specific. The task is to grow in appreciation of all that comes together to form the total heritage of any congregation.

## The Common Heritage

The starting point in celebrating one's heritage is to affirm what is shared with all other Christians as the common faith heritage. This central core of belief and experience belongs to Christians everywhere and in all ages. It is the base upon which all teaching of the church is built and by which teaching is tested.

Christians share the Bible as the church's book. In that book they find the story of God's self-revelation and mighty acts. It records the salvation story of how God has loved, redeemed, and restored to relationship an alienated humanity. It gives the account of God's supreme revelation in the life, death, and resurrection of Jesus Christ. It reveals the ministry of the Holy Spirit both in the lives of individuals and the community of faith called the church. All this and more belong to the whole family of God. It is the faith heritage shared by all believers and followers of Jesus Christ.

In the church's teaching ministry it is imperative to lift up and celebrate this common heritage. Such celebration affirms oneness in Christ and the unity of the Body. It recognizes the fact that more unites various Christians than divides them. Celebration places the emphasis upon the essence of the faith rather than a distinction or peculiarity. It avoids the distortion that can easily emerge from excessive emphasis on what separates rather than unites. A total distortion of the gospel is possible when anyone makes a peripheral issue central in teaching. The safeguard against such error is to establish the common heritage of the Christian faith as the foundation of one's teaching ministry. Acknowledging the common faith heritage helps prevent the sin of self-pride. Groups that speak as though they have an exclusive claim on God's truth deceive themselves. There is motivation to have a more humble attitude when one recognizes that others share this common heritage.

## The Denominational Heritage

The heritage of one denomination is obviously different from that of another denomination, and yet so much is similar that it is possible to speak in general terms about what a denominational heritage means. The majority of all congregations identify with a denominational family. Some denominations are closely knit and maintain a tight measure of control over their churches. Others are loosely structured, and the individual congregations demonstrate a high degree of autonomy and independence. (The type of structure can be a significant factor in an individual's measure of comfort in the particular congregation. Persons will tend to identify with the type of congregation that is compatible with their personality types.) Not all denominational differences are rooted in major differences of belief or practice; frequently they are primarily a matter of style. An evidence of such style is the ease with which persons move among churches of varying denominational labels. Such ease may be an indication that little importance has been put upon the distinction of a particular heritage, resulting in relatively weak loyalties.

If the assumption is made that a particular denominational focus came into being for good and valid reasons, then that distinctive heritage should be highlighted as an important emphasis within the teaching ministry. Why did our particular kind of church family come into existence? What were the circumstances? What were the primary issues? Who were the key leaders? What were they trying to accomplish?

Excellent teaching questions like these stimulate one's curiosity and encourage probing into the past from which we have come. If we assume that something very important rallied our forebears, the issue for today is to understand how that historic emphasis still applies to the life of the church. Until that unique or particular heritage is fully understood and made our own, we are in no position to share it with the larger community of faith. The special contributions of the various parts of the body immeasurably enrich the whole. This is possible, however, only when each part struggles to know what it stands for and how who it is can bless and strengthen the larger family. In this respect the differences among denominations need to be highlighted and celebrated, not as qualities that divide and separate, but rather as qualities that give richness and fullness to the whole body.

The teaching emphasis of a particular heritage never ought to build walls to shut others out but should build bridges of understanding and appreciation. Emphasis is not upon what one has that others do not have but, rather, upon what one has to share with others. There can be justifiable pride in what one's denominational family has stood for as long as there is an openness and readiness to affirm what other denominational families celebrate as their particular heritages.

The study of a denominational heritage will include a number of significant elements. The first of these will be an acquaintance with "our story." Each denominational family has its own special history. There is a particular point in time when the group came into existence. The circumstances surrounding that beginning are significant. Understanding those roots is an important factor in establishing one's present identity. Every person who is part of a specific tradition ought to know at least the rudiments of the story of that tradition.

Second, through the years of the life of a denomination, significant men and women emerge as leaders. An important step in discovering and understanding one's heritage is to learn something about these leaders and other outstanding persons who have been part of it. Biographies of leaders ought to be part of the study of any heritage. Such leaders serve as role models and highlight the nature of a particular tradition.

In the third place, in the course of the history of most denominations, certain dates or events stand out, marking important decisions or actions. Persons need to know these important milestones if they are to gain a historical perspective about their denominational family. Often important decisions or actions are marked by these dates, and the course of history is established by them. These dates throw light upon the process by which the group has evolved its present identity. Significant dates, once they are established, can provide linkage with world history, promoting understanding of the relationship of the denomination to its historical context. It is always important to recognize that the church and its many parts have their setting in real history.

Fourth, a denomination characteristically has certain distinctive beliefs or doctrines. These may be unique or, as is more common, shared with other denominations. Frequently the distinction is a matter of the emphasis given to a specific teaching. For example, there are some denominations that have come to be known as "peace churches" because they place a major focus on teachings about peace. This does not mean that other churches have no concern for peace or fail to teach about peace but simply that peace issues are not a central focus for them. It is essential that persons be taught the specific beliefs or practices that their denomination has chosen to highlight. They will never understand their heritage until they understand the principles for which their forebears lived, fought, and in some cases even died. If a church is to be faithful to its own tradition, it obviously must teach its members what it holds as its distinctive beliefs.

As part of the whole body, denominations have made their special contributions to the life and mission of the whole church. These contributions need to be lifted up and celebrated as a significant part of one's heritage. If the denomination was or is a leader in the struggle for religious liberty, the abolition of slavery, the battle for civil rights, or the preservation of God's creation, such contributions ought to be celebrated. Persons understand their heritage more fully when they begin to be aware of examples of times when the witness and the labor of their churches effected change. The past gives a very important perspective to the present. Without the past, it is not really possible to appreciate the values of a particular tradition. Just as important, of course, is the development of a clear understanding of a denomination's current contributions to the total mission of the church. Part of the awareness of one's identity comes out of an appreciation for what one's denominational family can give to others.

Denominational heritage contributes significantly to the context of the teaching ministry. At the same time care must always be exercised to keep the particular aspects of denominational heritage in perspective. One's own heritage is best understood in relationship to the whole church's heritage.

## Congregational Heritage

Each member of a family is unique. This is also true of the congregations in any denominational family. They may be alike in many ways, but there is always that which makes each one special and unique. The heritage of a particular congregation is most immediate in the experiences of the members and most clearly gives the sense of identity. The average person more easily identifies with the local congregation than with an entity further removed from direct experience. A large part of the learning about heritage has to come in relationship to the local experience.

Every congregation has a history. That history has to do with the time and circumstances of its founding, the persons who were instrumental in providing the necessary leadership, the ups and downs that the years have brought, and times when significant issues were confronted. Characteristically not much attention is paid to this history except on special anniversary observances when it may be briefly reviewed. This scant attention is unfortunate because one's history is an important dimension of a congregation's heritage. Some steps can be taken to make members more conscious of this history. The story needs to be in easily available written form; the writing style needs to be interesting and attractive. If it can be in popular form, more persons will find it readable. Interest in history will be stimulated if excerpts from the form are used from time to time in the church paper or newsletter and illustrations incorporated occasionally in the minister's sermons. Attractive displays of photographs, another way of creating the awareness of history, can impressively tell a story. They are probably most effective when used in conjunction with some special observance or celebration. Other types of displays (e.g., artifacts) can help create interest in the past. The essential point is to select persons who recognize the importance of congregational history and will work at the task of developing awareness and understanding.

A great deal of heritage is related to a church building. The architecture of a building can be a testimony to what the church believes about the faith. Stained-glass windows may picture heroes of the Bible or events in church history, or they may be memorials to former members of the congregation. Occasionally there will be rooms that bear the name of an individual or family of the church. The stories that lie behind such memorials offer interesting and sometimes vital insights into the history of the congregation. If the church has a long history, there may well have been other church buildings that predate the current one. Pictures of these edifices can help to give a sense of history. If there have been relocations, these moves may tell something of changing relationships to the community.

In every congregation are names of certain men and women in its history who stand out because of their special contributions. Some may be pastors who served with particular distinction. Others may be lay persons who by their deep commitment and unique qualities were able to provide outstanding leadership in an aspect of the church's life and ministry. Such persons are worthy of recognition in the church's history. The current members are indebted to these stalwarts of the past. The heritage of any group is perhaps best understood in terms of the lives of the people who have carried key roles through the year. What a congregation is today reflects in large measure the stories of the men and women who have gone before.

The surge of interest in recent years in personal heritage has sent many persons searching out the history of their families. Persons have discovered that a deeper understanding of their roots brings a new dimension of meaning to their own identity. The same thing is true about the history of a church family in terms of its ability to bring a new depth of meaning to its identity. To know ourselves, we need to know the roots from which we have sprung.

## Heritage and Teaching

Heritage not only shapes us but also provides the reference points to guide our development. If we never learn from the past, we will repeat the mistakes of the past. The present and the future grow out of the past and are built upon it. The church's teaching ministry is always building on something that has gone before. The content of one's heritage provides invaluable points of reference against which to check planning. Testing whether a teaching is within the church's particular tradition is helpful to planning the teaching ministry. Evaluative criteria gleaned from one's heritage are useful in structuring an educational program. When a teaching or a practice appears to run contrary to a church's heritage, it is time to raise a serious question about its appropriateness. Heritage ought not to be the master of the church, but it can be an invaluable guide.

The church has a challenge in its ministry of teaching and learning to help people discover their basic heritage as Christians. People need to remember who they are and share the common stories and symbols of the faith. They need the opportunity to enrich this heritage with the contributions growing out of their own faith experience. With the common heritage must also be the particular heritage which is associated with a denominational family and ultimately with a single congregation.

Heritage is one of the foundations of the teaching ministry. It makes an impact upon our faith, our discipleship, our very lives.

# Postscript

We have reviewed the foundations of the church's educational ministry. If taken seriously, these basic precepts will serve as sure guides to a strong and effective educational program. They will help to keep our ministry rooted in the values that the church has affirmed through the centuries. They will give us confidence that our planning has a strong and sure base.

May our vision of the church as the teaching community be clear and certain, and may we build well upon the foundations so that the ministry of the teaching church may go forward with new power and effectiveness.

## Appendix 1

# Session Outlines for Group Study

The following session outlines are designed to assist a group in studying the eight chapters of this book. Each session follows a general pattern with an introductory activity, an exploration of the chapter theme, and a consideration of the possible implications. The outlines are brief and require that the group facilitator do additional planning for a session.

If the opportunity is not provided for a group experience, the outlines can serve as a guide for individual study and reflection.

### Chapter 1—The Concept of the Teaching Church

#### *Introduction*

1. Ask group members to list some of the common perceptions that the congregation has about the church's teaching ministry and then briefly discuss them.

2. Select three perceptions which could make a difference if they were strongly affirmed by the congregation.

#### *Exploration of Chapter*

1. Using the italicized phrases of the goal statement in the section "Goal of Ministry," chart the goal of the church's teaching ministry on newsprint.

2. Have the group reflect on the following questions:
   a. What might be considered the key phrase in the statement?
   b. What is God's role? our role?

c. What are the anticipated outcomes?

d. What in the statement is applicable to our situation? Can we accept it as a statement of the goal of our teaching ministry?

2. How can we make the congregation aware of the statement?

3. Examine the five functions of the teaching church as described under "Functions of the Teaching Church." After a discussion period, develop a list of the specific implications that might apply to the church's educational program.

### *Closing the Session*

1. Seek consensus on the one thing that would do the most to enhance the church's awareness of itself as a teaching church.

2. Close with brief circle of prayer focusing on the concern for the teaching ministry.

## Chapter 2—Jesus Christ: The Foundation

### *Introduction*

1. Read 1 Corinthians 3:11 and ask the group members to reflect on the ways they think of Jesus Christ as "foundation." Spend a few moments sharing the reflections.

2. Think of ways that the church witnesses to the centrality of Jesus Christ.

### *Exploration of Chapter*

1. Discuss some of the reasons why the claim that Christ is Lord may not seem as bold a claim today as it did in the first century.

2. Examine the model for ministry as exemplified in the person and work of Jesus Christ, and develop a model of ministry for the church today. What would such a ministry look like? What steps do we need to take to actualize it? To what degree do we already have it?

3. Rate on a scale of 1 (low) to 10 (high) the response of the congregation to the commission given by Christ to the church. To what degree is the teaching ministry in the church considered a priority? What steps would we have to take to make it a priority?

4. Reflect on ways that the ministry of the church can be holistic rather than fragmented.

### *Closing the Session*

1. Ask the group to share personal experiences of Jesus Christ as the center of the faith experience.

2. Spend a few moments in silent reflection and close with a brief circle of prayer.

## Chapter 3—The Biblical Foundation

### *Introduction*

1. Ask group members to think about the phrase "people of the Book." Talk about the images communicated by the phrase.

2. Think about the sacred writings of other faiths and how the Bible is like or unlike these other writings.

### *Exploration of Chapter*

1. Examine some of the problems that the Bible presents to its readers. Which of these seem to offer the most serious difficulties to the contemporary reader? How good a job does our educational program do in helping persons learn how to deal with these issues?

2. Discuss the tremendous differences that can emerge from the process of biblical interpretation. How can "right" interpretation ever be distinguished from "wrong" interpretation? Who determines what is normative?

3. Look at the suggested guides for interpreting Scripture. How are these applicable to the teaching program in our church? What are ways that our teachers could be helped with biblical interpretations?

### *Closing the Session*

1. Ask the group members to suggest ways in which the session's discussion is applicable to their own individual Bible study.

2. Share in brief prayers of thankfulness for the message of the Bible.

## Chapter 4—The Continuing Work of the Holy Spirit

### *Introduction*

1. Have the group reflect on occasions when they experienced the power of the Holy Spirit at work in their lives.

2. Discuss the impact life in the scientific age has on one's belief in the continuing work of the Spirit.

### *Exploration of Chapter*

1. Talk about the components of a good teaching-learning experience and how these may be reflected in our own church's educational program.

   a. In what ways is church education different from other education?

   b. What is the "plus" in the church's teaching ministry?

   c. Does the church understand the role of the Holy Spirit in its teaching program? How could its understanding be increased?

2. Examine the evidence of the Spirit's ministry in the teaching program of our church. In what ways are we aware of the work of the Spirit? What more could be done to enhance awareness?

3. Discuss the gifts for teaching and their contribution to a more effective teaching ministry. Consider ways in which they could be enhanced in the church.

### *Closing the Session*

1. Reflect on the following statement: "The Spirit is the teacher and the church the co-teacher."

2. Sing "Spirit of the Living God."

## Chapter 5—The Teaching-Learning Community

### *Introduction*

1. Have the group think about early remembrances of the church as a special fellowship of people.

2. Talk about some of those remembrances.

### *Exploration of Chapter*

1. Make a list of the elements necessary to have *koinonia* in the church. Reflect on whether this is a common or rare experience.

2. Discuss the role of small groups in relating persons to the larger community, calling upon insights from personal experience.

3. Examine the qualities that the redemptive community offers to persons and ask how well these qualities are being reflected in the church.

4. Think of some examples of unplanned learning that have taken

place in this church or in other churches we have known. Talk about any negative messages that the church may have communicated.

### *Closing the Session*

1. Reflect on one thing that could most enhance the development of *koinonia* in the church.

2. Share in a circle of prayer for the church as a community of love and concern.

## Chapter 6—The Teaching-Learning Process

### *Introduction*

1. Recall the church school teacher who made the greatest impression on you. What was the most outstanding quality or ability of that teacher?

2. Make a brief list of the qualities that a good teacher should possess.

### *Exploration of Chapter*

1. Compare the various approaches that can be made to teaching and the values that each approach brings to the teaching situation. What factors influence a teacher's choice of approach?

2. Explore the meaning of the concept of the "teacher-learner."

3. Discuss the reasons why the growth process seems to come to a halt for some adults.

4. Consider ways to improve the planning of the educational program.

5. Explore the procedures for making leadership a matter of priority in the church's ministry of teaching.

### *Closing the Session*

1. Think about the persons currently giving educational leadership and how they could be given more support and encouragement.

2. Pray for all the teachers and leaders in the educational program.

## Chapter 7—Worship and Celebration

### *Introduction*

1. Think about a moment or situation in which the presence and power of God were present in worship in a very particular way. Did it

change life in some way?

2. Share some of those experiences.

### *Exploration of Chapter*

1. Talk about how the Christian year provides significant opportunities for basic teaching about the faith. Are such opportunities being adequately used?

2. Reflect on the learning opportunities in the experiences of corporate worship through Scripture, music, prayer, and the sacraments.

3. Discuss the role of preaching in the ministry of teaching.

4. Examine the current worship patterns and practices in light of the suggested guidelines for worship.

### *Closing the Session*

1. Spend some quiet moments becoming aware of God's presence.

2. Share in a circle of prayer for the church as a worshiping community.

## Chapter 8—Faith Heritage

### *Introduction*

1. Ask the group members to share briefly the particular faith heritage in which they were born and raised.

2. Reflect on the degree of awareness the congregation now has about its heritage and tradition.

### *Exploration of Chapter*

1. Reflect on the fact of diversity as found in the body of Christ. List some of the possible benefits as well as some of the drawbacks resulting from this diversity.

2. Discuss how it might be possible to affirm and celebrate the common heritage of all Christians.

3. Test how much the group knows about its own denominational heritage. If the amount is deficient, is this a matter of concern? What can be done about it?

4. Examine the church's sense and awareness of its own history and identity. How much do members know about their church? Is there any

plan for helping persons grow in their appreciation of the church's heritage?

### *Closing the Session*

1. Share briefly about the relationship of heritage to the teaching ministry.
2. Conclude with a circle of prayer for one another and for the teaching church.

Appendix 2

# Bibliography


Bartlett, David L., *Paul's Vision for the Teaching Church.* Valley Forge: Judson Press, 1977.

Blazier, Kenneth, ed., *The Teaching Church at Work.* Valley Forge: Judson Press, 1980.

Bowman, Locke E., Jr., *Teaching Today: The Church's First Ministry.* Philadelphia: The Westminster Press, 1980.

Evans, David M., *The Pastor in a Teaching Church.* Valley Forge: Judson Press, 1983.

Evenson, C. Richard, *Foundations for Educational Ministry.* Philadelphia: Fortress Press, 1971.

Groome, Thomas H., *Christian Religious Education: Sharing Our Story and Vision.* New York: Harper and Row, Publishers Inc., 1980.

Heckman, Shirley, *On the Wings of a Butterfly: A Guide to Total Christian Education.* Elgin, Ill.: Brethren Press, 1981.

Jones, Stephen D., *Faith Shaping.* Valley Forge: Judson Press, 1980.

Miller, Randolph C., *The Theory of Christian Education Practice: How Theology Affects Christian Education.* Birmingham, Ala.: Religious Education Press, 1980.

O'Hare, Padraic, ed., *Tradition and Transformation in Religious Education.* Birmingham, Ala.: Religious Education Press, 1979.

Olson, Richard Allan, *The Pastor's Role in Educational Ministry.* Philadelphia: Fortress Press, 1973.

Palmer, Parker, *To Know As We Are Known: A Spirituality of Education.* New York: Harper and Row, Publishers, Inc., 1983.

Seymour, Jack L., and Miller, Donald E., *Contemporary Approaches to Christian Education.* Nashville: Abingdon Press, 1982.

Taylor, Marvin J., ed., *Foundations for Christian Education in an Era of Change.* Nashville: Abingdon Press, 1976.

Westerhoff, John, III, ed., *Who Are We? In Search of an Identity for Religious Education.* Birmingham, Ala.: Religious Education Press, 1978.